CU01455061

Guardian of the Road: A Devotional Anthology In Honor of Hermes

Edited by K. S. Roy

"Hermes"
by K.S. Roy

BIBLIOTHECA ALEXANDRINA

Copyright © 2012 by Neos Alexandrina

All rights reserved. No part of this book may be reproduced by any means or in any form whatsoever without written permission from the author(s), except for brief quotations embodied in literary articles or reviews. Copyright reverts to original authors after publication.

Table of Contents

Introduction

"Hermes, for to you beyond all other gods it is dearest to be man's companion, and listen to whom you will..."
Zeus to Hermes. The Iliad 24. 334 ff

For some of us, Hermes was the first god we encountered on our paths, directly or indirectly. True to his title as Messenger of the Gods, he may have only introduced us to another member of the pantheon before flying off on those winged sandals of his. Maybe he came to us in dreams, whispering in our ears, dancing playfully just out of our range of vision.

Maybe it was his stories we loved best in the myths when we first heard them as a child. Maybe we heard he was a god of luck, and sought him out to win his favor. Or maybe he was always there, all along, and we finally realized one day who he was. Perhaps some of us are still trying to figure that one out.

In this book, you will see Hermes through the eyes of those who have experienced his presence in our lives. Hermes is a truly multi-faceted deity, as you will see through the diverse perspectives of this collection of essays, poems and stories.

Hermes is a god of riddles. He can be as elusive as the wind, or as close as the coins jingling in our pockets. Whether you're just beginning to get to know him, or have been walking with him on the road for quite some time, you're sure to derive some enjoyment and enlightenment from this book.

May Hermes guard all your journeys and help you along whatever road you take!

K.S. Roy

Guardian of the Road
by K.S. Roy

Hermes, I call on thee
Guardian of the Road
See the stones I've left for you
Here by the wayside
And hear my prayer ...

Keep clear the skies
So that I may use the stars
To find my way

Keep my mind alert
That I may explore new horizons
And widen my experience

Keep my heart open
That I may offer help along the way
To those in need

Keep my wits sharp
That I may know friend from foe
And act accordingly

And keep my road safe
That I may journey onward
Under your divine protection.

To Hermes Enodios
by Jennifer Lawrence

Setting out on journeys
Always makes my heart flutter a little;
The excitement of packing, planning
My route, looking forward to whatever
Awaits me at the end.
Released for just a day or two from
The boundaries that normally
Circumscribe my life; I feel free
As I leave the familiar confines of home behind.
Before I go, I call your name, pour out wine,
Ask you to be with me at every step —
Guardian, guide, traveling companion.
I ask you to keep me safe as I travel:
Safe from accidents, safe from missteps,
Unharmed and whole when I reach my destination.
In my mind's eye, I can see how your worshippers
Once said the same prayers, ages ago:
The road dusty under their sandaled feet
As they trudged the well-worn paths —
To Athens, to Delphi, to Pheneos in Arcadia
Where your festivals were held.
Summer's heat haze hanging in the air,
And the bleating of goats in the fields
along their path as they made their way.
No goats on my path, but I look for your signs
As I travel: turtle, serpent, kerykeon
Splashed across the back of a truck
Ferrying medical supplies from warehouse to hospital.
Midway through my trip, I will pause at a rest stop
On the side of the road and seat myself on a rock

3

To nibble my lunch. Then, finished, I'll
pile up smaller stones on that larger one I chose for my
seat
to mark the spot where, just for a handful of minutes,
I rested in the shade of the trees overhead,
Sweat spangling my brow like those old travelers,
And thought of you as they did
Before resuming my journey.

Hermes Among Us
by Amanda Sioux Blake

Hermes walks among us
In dust-covered human guise
The God of Travelers
Anonymous
Seemingly ordinary
Some may never spare Him a second glance
A baseball cap covers His eerie green eyes
Mischief sparkles in those pools
Deep and hard as emerald shine

Hermes rides the subway
Beneath New York City streets
Do the riders see His emerald eyes
Watching them over the newspaper?

Hermes commutes to work
On trains, in cars
He's with us all.
He's the stranger in the next car
The person in the airplane seat ahead of you
You may recognize Him in a fellow travelers' eyes
Or you may never see His face

Be mindful of your actions
The way you treat your peers
Give a friendly nod as you cross the street
To the man crossing the other way
You will never know if he is just a man
Or the Companion of Man.
Hermes walks among us –
Treat us with respect.

Hymn to Hermes
by Solongo Dulaan

Hail Hermes full of grace
Your lily white hands wave wantonly in the wild wind
Your caduceus with its snakes entwined
Loops with easy movement by your side
Lithe limber lord we look to you as guide
To the Underworld and its fright
Yet trickster and fool find you welcome
Criminal and businessman are your bedfellows
Your mind races on flights of fancy
Thoughts and dreams of frivolity mellow
A tease and a buffoon
Yet you are the most serious of oracles
When winter draws the snow around the moon
Music you find a pastime, and dance
Yet scholarly pursuits as well, given the chance
Lady Fortuna is your friend
Apollo finds you a cheeky mate
Zeus smiles in proud embrace
Hermaphrodite is your subtle twin
Lord of Air, Lord of Light
Lord of Darkness, Lord of Night
We look to you for a happy heart, a full mind,
And wishes of prosperity

In Honor of Hermes – A Classicist's Plea
by Galina Krasskova

Sweet Son of Zeus,
fleet-footed and facile, cunning and wise,
utterly impossible to capture –
least of all with words —
please hear my prayer.

Silver-tongued Seducer,
Opener of every way,
Who unlocks the tongue
and sets the mind on fire,
grant me luck in language

for I am drowning in the flood of words
and long forgotten syntaxes I must learn.

Open my ears to the voices of the past.
Bring me beneath the bower of my ancestors' blessings.
Open my heart to the wonder of their words.
Untangle my thoughts,
Oh You Who are swifter than any thought,
and whisper the words of places past
into the architecture of my mind.

Oh God of Travelers,
ward well the linguistic road I walk.
Open the way before me
that I may learn – well and sure —
to honor You
in the tongues of the lands
that first birthed Your praises.

Ward me well against impiety, Gracious Lord,
so that I may honor You always.

I Sing of Hermes
by Michael Routery

I sing of Hermes,
son of Maia, grandson of Atlas,
cave-born son of Zeus, quick footed
cattle lifter boundary crosser
wild boy lyre maker
circuit breaker wing-sandal traveler
gift giver luck bearer.
Hail Hermes in the crossroads
and on the pavement gleaming.

Hidden Acrostic
by Jason Ross Inczauskis

Hermes, Great Clever-Minded God,
Sweet Messenger, bearing tidings fair.
Whenever you are near,
Everything is much more clear,
And the words we need to speak, they will be there!
That's just a gift that we receive within your care!

Hermes, Swift Message-Bearing God,
Ever moving, never holding still.
Reveal to us your arts,
Mischief-Maker, lift our hearts,
Every trick you play provides another thrill,
So we can learn the lessons that you would instill!

Hermes, Kind Spirit-Guiding God,
You walk with us, when we live or die.
From birth until our end,
We couldn't ask a better friend,
For you're always there to cheer us when we cry!
And when you come to take us home, with you we'll fly!
For you give a gift of love we can't deny!

Hymn to Hermes I
by Rebecca Buchanan

quicksilver jackrabbit
leaping
jumping
swift
winged blur
'cross mountains
canyons
seas
deserts
rivers
grassy plains
quicksilver
arc of mercury
starry heaven to
rolling earth to
misty deadlands
knife slicing 'cross creation
laughing

The Guide
by D.L. Wood

I go through these woods
Dark and without light
Tripping and slipping
Along my path,
Frightened and cold.
Lost.
I never knew the Way.
Then You --
Guide,
Teacher,
Mentor,
Friend --
You came to me,
Swiftly, as You do,
With no Fear.
No Doubt in me.
And a word of advice.
Heed it, You said, You will be Free.
Your whispers come in the night,
In the day, and in between.
When I am unsure,
My hand you take,
Guiding me back to Right.
You live in my thoughts.
You live in my breath.
In my words.
In my actions.
Smiling kindly,
You watch over me,
Helping me gain footing
On less solid ground.

Because of you
I have learned respect.
I have learned to Love.
I have learned the importance,
Of Truth.
I have learned.

Heliotrope Hedgerow
by Christa A. Bergerson

shall we now enter the thorny thicket
the floor of the woods so fully clothed
wicked roses strangling pale picket
how neatly the grass seems to be mowed

behind the heliotrope hedgerow lives
Hecate, a lady who surely knows
the vision of Hermes Trismegistus
and emerald tablets that ghost grass grows

follow her to the other side of time
visit the man with the thousand faces
better hurry to be the first in line
pray that you will be in his good graces

take the key and cross through the clover door
transcend sublunary forevermore

Prayer to Hermes for Counselors, Psychologists, and Mental Health Workers
by Sarenth Odinsson

Hail Holy Healer
Give me the words
To soothe the mind
Comfort the worried
Uplift the oppressed

Help me, Holy Healer
Untie the mind
Open the eyes
Waken the senses
Ease the pain

Bless me, Holy Healer
May my words speak truth
May my voice speak strength
May my heart beat courage
May my soul show faith

Thank you, Holy Healer
For the gift of my words
For the trust in my craft
For the honor of your work

Hymn to Hermes II
by Rebecca Buchanan

three hours into a seventeen hour drive
and the check engine light comes on
two thousand dollars to fix this problem
and I'm pissed
but not Hermes
he's a god who likes to fuck with people
the curveball
the wrench in the works
that's Hermes
laughing at how we complain and whine and stress
we little mortals
who can't see the whole thing is a game

For Hermes
by Ariana Dawnhawk

The words are uncertain,
chancy at best.
The magic doesn't always come out
the way I want it to.
The paths divide endlessly.
Night comes,
and out of it laughter
wild and knowing,
pouring the stories
the unasked-for gifts --
old voices
old messages
made new
give breath and flight
until I, too, can laugh.

To Hermes
by Amanda Sioux Blake

Of Hermes I sing, crafty Son of Zeus
The Trickster from Kyllene
Who wears the traveler's cloak
With wings at His feet
And mischief in His eyes
The wheels of His mind are ever turning
The swift-footed One, herald of the Gods
He rules over the forum, and all commerce
The God of thieves and honest businessmen alike
He is the God of boundaries – though no boundary can hold him
Shepherd God, lover of many nymphs
Father of Eternal Pan, Goat-Footed,
Who plays His pipes in the Arcadian woods
And Hermes Hypnos I sing, as well
Who shuts our eyes at night
And brings sweet sleep.
With Hekate, Khthonic Hermes rules over the art of magic
Sorcereous God, I praise You too.
All these aspects and more, I invoke.
Let there always be song and wine for the Great God Hermes.

Summoning Hermes Betwixt the Night
by Christa A. Bergerson

Somewhere deep beyond the hills of Arcadia
Cloaked by the darkened night
Travelers wait humbly beneath the herm

Chorus:
Oh wondrous lithe and spirited God
We call upon you with tender whispers

May you come forth in our silky dreams
With winged feet that barely touch the earth

We offer you four gifts
Firstly the sacred ram roasting in this pit

Come, drink from this silver chalice
Taste our honey and cinnamon elixir

We invite you to smell the libanom
Burning in the brass and turquoise censer

And our most precious offering
Panspermia not tasted by our lips

Oh Hermes
You are a guide among guides, the great rescuer
A watcher of shepherds and their herds

Oh Hermes
We pray for your guidance through this dank and treacherous
fortress
Where even the fearless dare to tread

Oh Hermes
We revere you as much more than a weaver of dreams, or a
cattle thief
You are handsome and a nimble athlete

Oh Hermes
You are cunning and brilliantly deceptive -- The Great God of
Oration
We bathe you in our forever loving adoration

The High Priest:
Be still and listen closely
I hear his helmet all aflutter

See how sly he moves
Betwixt the sublunary and nether realm

Step aside fellow travelers
It is best to not get caught in his sway
Now behold the mighty Psychopomp
The lucky messenger donning a winged cap

Arriving suddenly, Hermes tosses coins in the wind

He points his kerykeion
Where the seas crawl toward the horizon

Hermes:
I have words for you

I am like the dark stallion
Stealth is my only companion

It is true I have the gift beyond gifts

A passport granted by the deathless --
Those ancients who reign supreme

But do not call upon me with empty hearts and befuddled minds

Stand tall through your convictions
My only request is your everlasting submission

I'll take you where you wish
Leave your coins upon this dish

This road may lead you home
Although, there is no map which can take you back

The worshippers follow in obeisance

Hermes at the Gate
by Jennifer Lawrence

He stands there, waiting patiently for me,
A smile on his face, hat in his hands.
There is no dust from the road on his sandals yet
As he waits for me to come out and join him:
The journey -- our last one together --
Has not yet begun.
Always in the past, he has traveled with me,
Everywhere I went, on such long and grand voyages
As the one I made years ago to New York,
Or the one before that, with my brother, as a child,
To spend the summer with my mother in North Carolina,
While she was in the army (serving under Athena's
shield).
Small trips, too -- a walk through the park with my dog,
Watching her chase the geese while I rested
In the slant of a willow's trunk at the lake's edge,
Or even just a quick trip to the grocery store,
Where he would sometimes bless me with the gift
Of unexpected winnings or a dollar found on the
sidewalk.
But this, our last journey together --
I do not want to set out on this one,
The black road before me,
Not so long as I would like it to be
(Never-ending),
But coming to a stop before Hades' dark throne.
I tell myself I should not fear:
He has never let me come to harm before
On our journeys together,
But even so, I hesitate, reluctant to step out
To the gate to greet Him,

Perhaps because when this voyage is over,
I will never again walk dusty back roads in the summer sunlight,
Not talking, just living --
Being --
With Him at my side.

Hymn to Hermes III
by Rebecca Buchanan

he's never still
the fleet-footed one
ever moving
ever in motion
here to there
    to there
and back again
    again:
everything is interesting
and he has a universe to explore

"Hermes Angelos"
by D.L. Wood

Prayers to Hermes
by D.L. Wood

Lovely Messenger
Swiftly imparting knowledge
Patient Teacher and Dear Friend.
Hermes, of winged foot and cap
I pray to you
Please help me find the words
For this situation
Help me be confident
In speech and action
While I am speaking today.
Help me to communicate to others as they will best understand it.
Jokester Hermes,
Help me have humor
If I begin to take life too seriously
And find the lessons in all things,
Good or bad.
Help me apply the knowledge I have learned,
And guide me to sources of knowledge I need to learn.
Sweet and true,
Sayer of Soft Words.
Bringer of news,
Help me understand the messages
I am given today from the universe.
Help me to take what I need from these.
Inventor Hermes,
Help me to be creative when faced with problems today.
Celestial Hermes,
Protect me from all harm during travel,
That I may arrive at my destination and arrive home safely.

Protect the other travelers on the road,
That they may use good judgment while driving, and stay safe.
Psychopomp Hermes,
Thank you for guiding us, in daily life, and after.
Please help the souls of departed, or departing, find a peaceful journey home.
Magnificently Divine One,
I praise and honor you.

Neos Hermes, The Great Translator: Hermes, Antinous, and Syncretism
by P. Sufenas Virius Lupus

It is not without precedent in the ancient Greek world to equate a living human with a particular deity using the phrase *Neos* _____, with a deity's name in the blank. The most widespread such usage was *Neos Dionysos,* a title given to or adopted by various rulers from the Hellenistic era onwards, including the Ptolemies[1] and the philhellenic Roman Emperor Hadrian.[2] The youthful lover of the Emperor Hadrian, Antinous, became a god who was syncretized to a number of deities, including Dionysos. He was called by the Dionysian epithets *Antinous Choreios, Antinous Epiphanes,* and *Antinous Neos Iakkhos,*[3] but he was never called *Neos Dionysos.*[4] However, he was called *Antinous Neos Hermes* on at least one surviving occasion, and his connections to Hermes through syncretism are abundant otherwise.[5]

I know of no other living or former human who was given the title *Neos Hermes,* so it might be interesting to investigate this matter further and probe what, exactly, the designation Neos Hermes means, not only in the case of Antinous, but what it could mean more widely, and particularly what it might herald for the entire notion of syncretism. Therefore, the present discussion will first outline the syncretistic connections between Antinous and Hermes, and will then proceed on to examine what this syncretism, if it were to be applied elsewhere or more widely, might indicate.

The inscription that names Antinous as *Neos Hermes* comes from Rome, and is written in Greek, and dedicated by a group of people represented by one

Nikias, who together with his group "stand[s] in awe of the beautiful Antinous" and raises him as "the New God Hermes."[6] The date of this inscription is uncertain, but it likely comes from some period around the middle of the second century CE, since Antinous' death was in October of 130 CE, and his worship was particularly active in the Antonine Period (the reigns of Hadrian through Commodus), though it also lasted through the third century and into the fourth as well. Antinous' heritage connected him to Arcadia, and while Antinous was also syncretized with the god Pan, Hermes was both Pan's father and was one of Arcadia's principal deities as well.[7] It has been suggested by both Caroline Vout[8] and J. R. Rea[9] that because Antinous' death by drowning took place in the vicinity of Hermopolis in Egypt, that this may account for his syncretism to Hermes; however, his Arcadian connections through both his genetic heritage and his name (as Antinous is the masculine form of the name Antinoë, the foundress of the Arcadian city-state of Mantineia, from which Antinous' home city of Bithynion-Claudiopolis was a colony) would very likely have suggested the syncretism otherwise.

Several other sources for the syncretism of Antinous to Hermes occur in Egypt. Alexandria issued a number of coins that depict a profile bust of Antinous with a small lotus-flower crown on the obverse, with a horse-mounted Antinous as Hermes bearing a cadeuceus on the reverse.[10] A poem written for Hadrian in the immediate aftermath of Antinous' death, called *Periegete* by Dionysius of Alexandria, has an acrostic in it which reads "To The God Hermes Under Hadrian," which is an allusion to Antinous.[11] At Oxyrhynchus, a fragmentary encomium to Hermes and Antinous has been discovered as well from the third or fourth century.[12] An epic poem fragment also found at Oxyrhynchus, conjecturally attributed to Pancrates/Pachrates of Heliopolis, names Antinous as "son of the Argus-slayer" (*Argeiphontes*), which is to say, Hermes.[13] A further fragmentary hymn from Oxyrhynchus dating to the time of Diocletian's accession in the late third century CE also seems to name Antinous as the son of Hermes in some capacity.[14] In other Egyptian documents, the double theophoric name Hermantinous is attested.[15] While the syncretism of Antinous and Osiris seems to be the most sensible and appropriate to Egypt, it seems that Antinous as Hermes was also quite widespread there as well.

A further piece of evidence links Antinous to Hermes in an unexpected location: Delphi. Both Apollon and Dionysos have significance and are celebrated in Delphi, and Antinous is certainly connected to both of them—the former in the epithet *Neos Pythios* that occurs on some of his coins, but these all come from Asia Minor.[16] In Delphi, there are a series of coin issues that are distinguished by the epithet attached to Antinous being *Heros Propylaios*, "Hero Before-the-Gates,"[17] which, though it can be applied to Apollon, and perhaps to the Delphic hero Autonoös,[18] is generally a Hermetic epithet.

Karl Kerényi, writing of this Hermetic epithet, notes that it appears on a statue of Hermes in the Propylaion near the Acropolis in Athens, and that common folk usage said that this *propylaios* statue was said to be *amuetos*, "not a participant in the mysteries"; while elsewhere, a copy of this statue in Pergamum had the inscription GNOTHI SAUTON, "Know Thyself," upon it, thus hearkening back to the Delphic Maxims.[19] This series of relationships suggests, at least to me, a possible set of meanings that could be applied to

Antinous as *Heros Propylaios.* If Hermes is "not a participant in the mysteries," then it either suggests that he is outside of or excluded from them for some reason, or that he need not participate in them because he has been initiated already. As a psychopomp, my suspicion is more the latter than the former, as the foremost mysteries in the Greek world — those of Eleusis — were mysteries of death and rebirth, and Hermes was an essential operative in those, both in the myth of Persephone's return to her mother Demeter,[20] and to the transition from life to death generally speaking. And to "Know Thyself" could equally mean two things: to know that one is mortal and therefore prone to imperfection, error, and death, but also to know that one's deepest nature is divine. This accords well with another set of mysteries, those of Dionysos and of Orpheus, in which many of the inscribed texts that were buried with initiates had phrases on them that stated "I am a child of Earth (Gaia) and starry Heaven (Ouranos), but my soul is of Heaven alone,"[21] thus conveying the human condition of mortality despite divinity. Connecting this set of imagery and interpretations to Antinous, one of the most famous historical mortals to have become a deity, through these various connections to Hermes, seems both logical and appropriate.

Antinous appears in various guises of Hermes on many of the coin issue reverses featuring him.[22] Coins generally speaking are Hermetic in character, as Hermes/Mercury was a god of commerce. Hermes Nomios, "the herdsman," or, perhaps even "the good shepherd," is one such aspect under which Antinous appears. I would liken this to *Hermes Psychopompos* as well, as the "guide of souls" in the afterlife corresponds to various guides of souls during life, including the

31

"pastoral" function suggested by the shepherding metaphor. In Mantineia, the Arcadian city of Antinous' ethnic origin, and which was connected to Hermes in that his son Pan (another shepherd deity) was said to have been born there,[23] Antinous is honored in various ways, including in an inscription in which grieving parents dedicated their son's protection to Antinous in a manner suggesting his psychopomp nature.[24] Lying behind all of these matters, Antinous had mysteries celebrated in his honor, which probably had something to do with overcoming death; and, to connect this back into the *Heros Propylaios* relationships mentioned above, he would have "stood outside" of these mysteries, since he was not a recipient of them so much as the first mystagogue, the first revealer of and leader through, them.

But, leaving the matters of potential afterlives and deification behind, what are the significances of Hermes' syncretistic connections to Antinous for people in this life? I would like to suggest — and, to suggest conjecturally and theologically, whereas the previous discussion has been largely descriptive and therefore more definite — that the significance of Antinous being the *Neos Hermes* gives many clues into the process of syncretism itself.

Let us consider some of the ways in which Hermes and his connections play into this suggestion. Hermes is, as mentioned previously, a god of commerce, as well as a psychopomp. He is the messenger of the gods, and the inventor of language. He is a slayer of all-seeing monsters (though some have suggested that Argeiphontes suggests instead that he was a slayer of hounds),[25] and the foremost thief and liar[26] (in addition to the inventor of the lyre!). Hermes' very name is found within the science and the procedural methodologies of interpretation, hermeneutics, including in its original Greek root meaning "interpretation" (*hermeneusis*). On a very fundamental level, Hermes is a god of communication, of transition, and of translation.

Syncretism — whether it happens between pantheons and cultures, or within them — is also a process of exchange, communication, and translation. Through names and epithets — the domain of *Hermes Logios* — it can often occur. Like coinage, new syncretisms can be centrally issued or "struck," and then distributed widely, or a syncretism can be local and patronized on a smaller level. Such syncretisms can be a medium of cultural exchange, and even of cultural capital, that allow different communities to connect with one another, as well as for humans of diverse groups to better connect with the gods. Taking up the image or the epithet of an already-existing deity is a borrowing, in a sense, but it could also be understood as a kind of benign theft as well — something else which Hermes excels at, even to the point of convincing those from whom he has stolen through persuasive speech (and even outright lies) that he is innocent of such an offense. Neither the gates of Hades nor the fiercest and most ferocious monsters can resist his advances, either.

If the Argus-Slayer is the father (whether literal or metaphorical) of Antinous, then it seems that he taught all of these skills and lessons to his son, who is one of the most promiscuously syncretistic deities that has ever been known to exist in the Graeco-Roman-Egyptian world. He has stolen the names, the images, and the epithets of many deities, and has done so in such a sweet and benevolent fashion that none of the gods have seemed to object to it. He has inspired beautiful poetry, hymns, and other workings of words in devotees from soon after his death right down to the present, and the interpretations that these writings create of both Antinous himself and of theological realities generally is the very essence of *hermeneusis*. And, he has done all of this as a way to guide souls through the trials of their lives and into the mysteries of their afterlives as well. If there is any figure throughout history who is more deserving of the title *Neos Hermes* than Antinous, I do not know who it would be, personally.

Very interestingly, it is Hermes (or, in his Roman syncretism, Mercury) who is the kind of "master key" of syncretism for so many other deities in other cultures. As one prominent example, I would cite the "Gaulish Mercury" identified by Julius Caesar as the foremost deity of the Gauls, who is probably to be identified with Lugus, a deity who is related to Lug in Ireland and both Lleu and Llewellys in Wales.[27] Lug in particular is one of the most multi-functional gods imaginable, particularly amongst Celtic cultures, which have so many deities who have a wide variety of associations and affinities. It makes sense, therefore, that Hermes (under Mercury's name) would be the bridge to this further world of multivalent connections through syncretism.

The Greek term *metaphor* is an important concept in understanding myth, magic, religion, art, poetry, rhetoric, language, and a great many other areas of life. The exact linguistic equivalent of this term in Latin is *translatio*, the root of the English word "translation." Both *metaphor* and *translatio* mean "to carry over" or "to take across." When one translates something linguistically, one carries the meaning of a text in one language over into a sensible form in another language. Metaphors, through the very medium of language itself, likewise use a potent image to give a particular analogous meaning further color and impact in its usage. Translation and use of metaphors both involve interpretation, which is another exercise in the carrying over of one set of meanings into another context or environment for ease of understanding. And syncretism is perhaps one of the most advanced and involved employments of translation, interpretation, and metaphor that can be imagined. The act of *hermeneusis*, of hermeneutics, of the very art of Hermes, is an essential part of all of these activities. Even the most casual use of language is a stealing from the treasure-house of words bequeathed to a particular culture and all of the individuals in it, in order to put ideas into a particular order that will convey certain meanings and guide the thoughts of the linguistic production's audience in a particular direction — it is a guiding and leading of souls, as it were, whether it is on a journey of ecstatic heights in artistic exultation, a mere conveying of information, or the subtle process of seduction utilized by advertisers to both lie and tell the truth in order to get people to buy their clients' products. I would conjecture that Hermes, and Antinous as one of the foremost gods of syncretism, are both intimately tied up with these sorts of activities, and understanding them is inextricable from understanding the very roots of language and interpretation themselves.

Even if one only accepts the reality of the gods as metaphors, as archetypes, as symbols (which I do not!), then one must nonetheless marvel that the very force that makes such an interpretation of the gods possible, both in interpreting them in this fashion and in understanding them as metaphorical, is a process in which Hermes' nimble fingers, subtle words, and fleet feet are so involved that it would be difficult to deny his reality as a being of both true messages and confounding lies even while trying to argue for the validity of "mere metaphors" as acceptable theological interpretations of the gods. Where any two things exist — be they subatomic particles, humans, or a human and a deity, and everything in between and beyond these possibilities — then the communication and interaction between them must take some sensible form, and that form, I would suggest, is in the forum of Hermes. Karl Kerényi suggests that between the characters of Dionysos and the Dionysian, and Apollon and the Apollonian, which are often posited as a basic duality in spirituality, there is a third, mediating force, which is Hermes and the Hermetic[28] (though not necessarily in the late antique Graeco-Egyptian theurgic sense). It makes sense, therefore, that a figure as syncretistic as Antinous is syncretized not only to the chthonic Dionysos and the celestial Apollon, but to the mediating force of Hermes as well — and Hermes in particularly multiform and persistent forms. Antinous is not the *Neos Dionysos*, only the *Neos Iakkhos* as a young god of the mysteries; he is not the *Neos Apollon*, only the *Neos Pythios* as a god of oracles; but in addition to being the son of the Argus-Slayer, Antinous is the *Neos Hermes* most of all.

Syncretism and polytheism, in my mind, are unavoidable and inseparable. We live in a multicultural world, and thus syncretism will have to be a reality within it; and as polytheists, the pluriformity of deities ever increases, but must often be mediated by syncretism in some form or another. In speculating about the nature of polytheistic theology, David L. Miller writes,

A polytheistic theology will be stories of the gods (rather than theistic systems) and an aesthetic creation (rather than a logic of life). It will be theopoeisis .... A polytheistic theology will be a theology of the word, but in the manner of Hermes, who is appointed messenger of the Gods because he promises never to lie, but adds that it may be necessary for him not to tell the truth in order that he may not lie. Hermes was a trickster.[29]

With mythology, metaphor, theology, language, poetry, and polytheism in general, I expect that Hermes and Antinous, therefore, will be quite active in the near future, as polytheism takes root in the hearts and minds of more and more people. The re-interpretation of old stories, the creation of new ones, and the understandings that all flow from these are entirely within the sphere and are wholly in the realm of influence of Hermes, the great translator, the prime mover of metaphors, whose very name is the essence of interpretation itself. For any *Neos Hermes* to tap into such a primal and yet pragmatic force, whether it be Antinous or some other yet unidentified, unknown, or still-to-be-revealed figure, is to hold the master key to open a world of infinite possibilities in syncretism, in interpretation, and into language and communication on their most basic but most powerful levels.

Notes

1. Walter Burkert, "Bacchic *Teletai* in the Hellenistic age," in Thomas H. Carpenter and Christopher A. Faraone (eds.), *Masks of Dionysus* (Ithaca and London: Cornell University Press, 1993), pp. 259-275.

2. Henri Stierlin, *The Roman Empire: From the Etruscans to the Decline of the Roman Empire* (Cologne: Taschen, 2002), pp. 162, 165.

3. P. Sufenas Virius Lupus, *The Syncretisms of Antinous* (Anacortes: The Red Lotus Library, 2010), pp. 18-22.

4. Antinous is also called *Neos Pythios*, an Apollonian epithet, on some coin issues.

5. Lupus, *Syncretisms*, pp. 14-17; *Devotio Antinoo: The Doctor's Notes, Volume One* (Anacortes: The Red Lotus Library, 2011), pp. 207-208.

6. Hugo Meyer, *Antinoos: Die archäologischen Denkmäler unter Einbeziehung des numismatischen und epigraphischen Materials sowie der literarischen Nachrichten, Ein Beitrag zur Kunst- und Kulturgeschichte der hadrianisch-frühantoninischen Zeit* (Munich: Wilhelm Fink, 1991), pp. 169-170; translated in Lupus, *Devotio Antinoo*, p. 425.

7. Lupus, "From Arcadia with Love: Pan and the Cult of Antinous," in Diotima et al. (eds.), *Out of Arcadia: A Devotional Anthology for Pan* (Bibliotheca Alexandrina, 2011), pp. 86-93.

8. Caroline Vout, *Power and Eroticism in Imperial Rome* (Cambridge: Cambridge University Press, 2007), p. 132n176.

9. J. R. Rea (ed.), *The Oxyrhynchus Papyri* 63 (London: Egypt Exploration Society, 1996), §4352, pp. 1-17 at 10.

10. Gustav Blum, "Numismatique d'Antinoos," *Journal International d"Archéologie Numismatique* 16 (1914), pp. 33-70 at 53-57.

11. Kai Broderson (ed./trans.), *Dionysios von Alexandria, Das Lied von der Welt* (Hildesheim: Georg Olms AG, 1994), pp. 74-77 lines 513-532; translated in

Lupus, *The Phillupic Hymns* (Eugene: Bibliotheca Alexandrina, 2008), pp. 135, 263-264; *Devotio Antinoo*, pp. 385-387.

12. P. J. Parsons, "Hexameter Verse: Ethopoea and Encomium," in A. K. Bowman, H. M. Cockle *et al.* (eds.), *The Oxyrhynchus Papyri* 50 (London: Egypt Exploration Society, 1983), §3537, pp. 59-66. One day, I hope to produce a translation of what remains of this text, with the lacunae filled in with something conjectural but appropriate; it is beyond my means to do so at present, however.

13. Arthur S. Hunt (ed.), *The Oxyrhynchus Papyri* 8 (London: Egypt Exploration Society, 1911), pp. 73-77 at 75.

14. Rea, p. 10.

15. *Ibid.*

16. Blum, pp. 52-53.

17. Meyer, pp. 170-171.

18. From Herodotus 8.39; see Robin Waterfield (trans.), *Herodotus, The Histories* (New York and Oxford: Oxford University Press, 1998), pp. 500-501.

19. Karl Kerényi, *Hermes Guide of Souls*, trans. Murray Stein (Putnam, CT: Spring Publications, 1976), p. 121.

20. See the "Homeric Hymn to Demeter"; Apostolos N. Athanassakis (trans.), *The Homeric Hymns* (Baltimore and London: The Johns Hopkins University Press, 1976), pp. 11-12, in which Hermes is mostly called *Argeiphontes* ("Argus-Slayer") in the process of his being sent to negotiate with Hades for the return of Persephone, and then his escorting of her back to Demeter. Further, for the idea of "already" being an initiate or knowledgeable about what the mysteries

contain, in relation to Antinous specifically, see my essay in Melitta Benu et al. (eds.), *Queen of the Sacred Way: A Devotional Anthology for Persephone* (Bibliotheca Alexandrina, 2012), and the text attributed to Herakles in the Tebtynis Papyrus, translated in Lupus, *Devotio Antinoo*, pp. 366-369; and in *The Phillupic Hymns*, pp. 54-55.

21. Fritz Graf and Sarah Iles Johnston, *Ritual Texts for the Afterlife: Orpheus and the Bacchic Gold Tablets* (London and New York: Routledge, 2007), pp. 4-7, 16-17, 20-29, 34-35, 40-41.

22. Blum, *passim*.

23. Sir James George Frazer (trans.), *Apollodorus, The Library*, 2 Volumes (Cambridge: Harvard University Press, 1921), Vol. 2, pp. 304-305 (Epitome vii.38).

24. Vout, p. 123n137.

25. M. L. West (ed.), *Hesiod, Works & Days* (Oxford: Oxford University Press, 1978), pp. 368-369.

26. Norman O. Brown, *Hermes the Thief: The Evolution of a Myth* (Great Barrington, MA: Lindisfarne Press, 1990).

27. For an extended discussion of this, and several other Continental and Insular Celtic deities connected to language and warrior activites, see Phillip A. Bernahrdt-House, "Warriors, Wisdom and Wood: Oral and Literary Magic in the Exploits of Irish Mythological Warriors," *Studia Celtic Fennica* 6 (2009), pp. 5-19.

28. Kerényi, p. 23.

29. David L. Miller, *The New Polytheism* (Dallas: Spring Publications Inc., 1981), p. 90.

To Hermes at the Crossroads of Earth and Sky, Also Known As O'Hare
by Ariana Dawnhawk

We came spiraling down the path
Guided by the right information,
this time.
From car to bus to home
in the nick of time
we arrived
Tracing our way
from secrets and magic
along the street of curry (and others)
to hotels upon hotels
Faster than we hoped --
Hermes, thank you.

Hymn to Hermes IV
By Rebecca Buchanan

merry
laughing-eyed
lord of mischief:
your joy is a gift
that I return in kind

The Naming
By Melia Suez

Well as they say, wee one, when a door closes, a
window opens.... Not that anyone could keep me out if I
truly wanted in. Hush now. Poor tyke. It's just our dear
old dad is venting his anger. He's pretty upset over
having to let you go Yet Olympus ... well it is no place
for a child. Any child. And there is Hera to consider ....
I practically had to pry his hands open, to get you away
in time. Get that ivy out of your mouth, belly aches are
no fun. Out of his thigh, you came, your father is your
mother, too. Something no male, mortal or divine, has
ever done. Or will ever do again. But Hera left him with
no choice. This is your third go around, Dad refused to
lose you yet again, Afraid the Fates would not allow
another attempt, I bet. That was a dastardly trick she
played on your ma. Ah now, don't cry. You will see her
again. I promise. When you are old enough, when
you're able enough I will tell you what to do and how to
do it. We'll beat that grumpy old queen, yet. But first,
you need a name, bro. Dad said to take you to Mount
Nysa. Nysa. I like it. Wait. Nysa sounds too feminine....
Nysos. I'll call you Nysos. Ah, there you are
ladies. Nysos, these are the rainy ladies of Nysa. Ladies
this is your charge, the child of Dios, Nysos. No, no,
don't thank me, just take the babe and keep him hidden.
Hera will be looking for him soon. I'll be back when I
can. I will have to make other arrangements first. Got to
fly! Things to do, places to go!

What did he call him? That Hermes is always in
such a rush. What are we going to do with a baby?
Dionysos, I think. He was speaking so fast....

43

Dionysos and Hermes
by P. Sufenas Virius Lupus

I remember back when I snatched him from heaven's
    fires;
into Nysian nymphs' hands I conveyed him
when as a goat he was saved from Ino and Athamas;
but never have I seen him in a sadder state.

As ever, he is young and beautiful,
the desire and object of every eye that beholds him,
his long blond-streaked hair glistening,
people calling him "Miss" despite his dark stubble.

I look at him now through strange eyes:
in foreign flesh he resides, trapped, unknowing.

I am older, taller, nowhere near as thin,
a Silenos compared to his slimness,
I am balding like the Gaulish Ogmios
yet still as skilled in speech and quick-minded.

He wears a green shirt without sleeves,
the name of some rainbow-lettered cocktail lounge on
    his breast;
he is a slave to dragons, to liquids in bottles,
he stumbles not knowing the depths of his blindness.

Not even the Great Mother can cure him
of this blindness, twice as dangerous as Hera's madness;
I must take him to an unknown spring
where, bathing, he will have his sight restored.

But he fears swimming, and sitting behind a car's wheel,
and he has no trust in fit fleetness of foot.

I have seen how he might be healed,
his blindness restored to the rejoicing of all,
how his dancing feet might float upon the winds
and make prison doors swing wide open again.

I know what words will be in my mouth
on that festival when he returns to his senses,
how these lips will say "Do not give thanks to me,
rather thank the gods who have made it so."

He will lean on a new thyrsus of freedom's hues,
with lights shining for the illumination of many,
like a new Pharos guiding the sea-tossed ships
safely into welcoming ports of celebration.

But those revels are far in coming,
for he has forgotten his deepest nature.

Ever it has been the theme of his drama:
those who refuse the god are destroyed by him.
Dionysos has left the body where once he dwelt,
even as my awareness departs this borrowed one.

I lament for the loss that none will know has happened,
how the world has been deprived of a new Dionysos.
The blind and doubting shell left where he lived
will only be valued for his phallic endowments.

He has drank the grapes, but in being crushed like them he has not fermented and found new life as spirit; he has refused the cup, while overindulging the drink, and his screams while being stomped have been lost in the noise.

Hermes Kriophoros: An Aries' Prayer
by K.S. Roy

I thank you, Hermes
For carrying this little ram
On your shoulders
During all those times
When I felt more like a lamb ....

Born under the sign of the ram
But ruled by your star
I've followed you through dreams
Heard your whispers
Just behind my ear

We've journeyed together
For miles upon miles
From the northern mountains
And back again, to arrive
At the city that bears your name

I honor you who kept me safe
On dark roads and long nights
You who protected me
Against all dangers
Real and imagined

I honor you who guided me
To roads I would've never thought to follow
To ideas that seemed impossible
Lending me a little of your luck
Encouraging my curiosity

Please stay with me
And show me the way
Now and always
Guarding your little lamb
Who dares to become a ram.

A Kriophoria Ritual (For Groups)
by Amanda Sioux Blake

Barley Offering
Sprinkle barley on the altar, saying:
> To the givers of life, Life.

Purify the Circle
walk around the ritual space with the khernips bowl, sprinkling the water around the perimeter. Say:
> You are pure! You are pure! By this holy water, this ground is made pure. In the name of Apollo the Purifier this place is cleansed, and is now a holy sanctuary.

Walk in another circle, taking the bowl to each of the worshippers, so they can wash their face and hands. As they are doing so, say:
> By this holy water, you are made pure. In the name the Apollo the Purifier, you are holy and fit to enter the Temple.

Intro
Today we gather to celebrate the Kriophoria, the Ram-Bearing Festival, in honor of the Great God Hermes. Today our ancestors honored Him as the guardian of flocks and fields, the shepherd's God. We are not shepherds anymore, but the sheep stand for all our wealth, both literal and metaphorical. We appeal to Hermes today as the God of all economies, of everything that has value.

Orphic Hymn To Hermes

Hermes, draw near, and to my prayer incline,
messenger of Zeus, and Maia's son divine;
prefect of contests, ruler of mankind,
with heart almighty, and a prudent mind.
Celestial messenger of various skill,
whose powerful arts could watchful Argos kill.
With winged feet 'tis thine through air to course,
O friend of man, and prophet of discourse;
great life-supporter, to rejoice is thine
in arts gymnastic, and in fraud divine.
With power endued all language to explain,
of care the loosener, and the source of gain.
Whose hand contains of blameless peace the rod,
Caduceus, blessed, profitable God.
Of various speech, whose aid in works we find,
and in necessities to mortal kind.
Dire weapon of the tongue, which men revere,
be present, Hermes, and thy suppliant hear;
assist my works, conclude my life with peace,
give graceful speech, and memory's increase.

To Hermes

Of Hermes I sing, crafty Son of Zeus
The Trickster from Kyllene
Who wears the traveler's cloak
With wings at His feet
And mischief in His eyes
The wheels of His mind are ever turning
The swift-footed One, herald of the Gods

He rules over the forum, and all commerce
The God of thieves and honest businessmen alike
He is the God of boundaries – though no boundary can hold him
Shepherd God, lover of many nymphs
Father of Eternal Pan, Goat-Footed,
Who plays His pipes in the Arcadian woods
And Hermes Hypnos I sing, as well
Who shuts our eyes at night
And brings sweet sleep.
With Hekate, Khthonic Hermes rules over the art of magic
Sorcereous God, I praise You too.
All these aspects and more, I invoke.
Let there always be song and wine for the Great God Hermes.

Offerings

Great Hermes, we bring You offerings of delicious food, of life-giving bread and coconut shrimp.
We welcome You to feast with us tonight. May it please You, as You bring joy to our hearts.

Hymn to Hermes V
by Rebecca Buchanan

he is honey-tongued
eloquence, charm
incarnate,
clever,
sly

"Hermes Psychopompos"
by D.L. Wood

Hermes' Temple
by D.L. Wood

The Sun rising in the East.
As the Cock crows, I exit my home,
Armed with Reverence and a Steady Heart,
My Mind on one goal ... For it is Wednesday ....

I make the familiar trek down the dirt path.
This is the home of Your nymphs.
They play with me as I walk to You.

Mount Cyllene ... beautiful, breathtaking.
I walk up the mountainside in the wooded morning
    sunlight
Adoring nature ...
... the light breeze against my cheek.

Every breath reminds me of my goal today.
Mindfully and purposefully I walk,
Tired as I am, and,
Enduring this path ...
This Moment is for You.

Deep within this place ....
Finally, I arrive.
This, Your Temple:
Marble steps hidden by growing moss and time ....

There is a clearing here.
Archaic columns take the place of trees.
Taking off my well-worn leather sandals,
I move inside, conscious of the cold marble floor.

Luminous torches line the walls ....
I am silent,
For You, Lord of Knowledge,
Arkadian One.

I kneel, slowly, with intent,
Closing my eyes ....
Your magic lives here.
Your energy comes gently,
Like a sparkling ray of sun.

I place my offering before Your blessed winged feet:
A quill I've made for You,
A blossom of spring,
Frankincense, which I light for You ....
I look up.

The wind blows through this ...
Hallowed, secret place,
Clearing away doubt ...
Fear is not welcome in Your home.

Clarity settles into mind,
Previously wrecked with care.
I touch your image, Your hand ....
One last thing;

Departing;
The wind follows me, beckoning.
Within my Heart I feel you, Messenger of the Gods.

Walking with me, ...
Holding my hand.
Returning a gift for a gift.

115th avenue off-ramp Denver 4 April 10:33 pm
by Rebecca Buchanan

hermes
i don't know you
you probably don't know me either
but my sister talked about you a lot
melanie
you should know her
she had your name tattooed across her heart
dad freaked
not that he could do anything about it
anyway she's gone now
but you probably know that
she said you take the dead to the afterlife
you better have taken her to a nice place
anyway melanie is why i'm here
i built this road
she died on a road like this one
she used to tell me that you watched over roads
you were the first one to walk the path
opening the way she called it
and then you watched over everyone
who used the road after that
you didn't watch over melanie
i don't know why
but i know there are lots of other girls out there
sisters like melanie
with brothers like me
and dads
so here i am
asking you to watch over this road that i built
and everyone who travels on it
and

if you could
carry a message to melanie too
(she said you do that)
tell her that her brother and her dad
really miss her
thanks

Westwards*
By Hélio Pires
Dedicated to Mercury and all the stray dogs

Ferdie was a dog like any other dog. He could jump, run, bark, stretch out his paws, and had an amazing sense of smell. He felt pain and love, two things he experienced with his old owners, who used to make him feel part of the family until they abandoned him by a dusty road. Ferdie ran after the car and barked, but to no avail. He wandered for days, searched frenetically in every crowd he came across, always hoping to find his family just around the corner. And every time he ended up alone. Yelping followed, usually with memories of the days when he used to be part of something. He remembered his toys, the soft bed, and the warm hug of a human. And food! All the things he'd lost, all the things he missed. If it hadn't been for his instincts and the occasional generosity from a stranger, Ferdie would be dead by now. He tried to stick to the people who helped him, hoping they would take him. He saw some of them had dogs of their own and that reminded him even more of his old life. And every time he was rejected, he yelped until sleep came to grant him a few moments of forgetfulness.

Ferdie lived like this for a year. Lost and alone, he ended up in the outskirts of Lisbon. He wanted to avoid the big city, because he knew the dangers in it. He heard about them from other stray dogs he'd met. Some vanished never to be seen again and others were killed on the streets. Ferdie had memories of big cities he visited with his old owners, so he had an idea of what the other dogs told him. But he also knew that there were more people there, which meant more chances of finding food and maybe a new family. Hope! People tend to think of it as a very human thing, as if only they could feel it. But dogs have it, too. Ferdie had it, even if he'd lost it for several moments in the last year. People go through that as well, but hope always comes back and sometimes makes you do things that may change your life. And that was the case when he found himself facing the big city. So Ferdie took a deep breath, closed his eyes for a few seconds, and walked into Lisbon.

It didn't take him long to make sense of the place. He quickly understood that the major streets were far too dangerous: too many people, too many cars, and too many chances of getting hurt or killed. He'd seen it happen to other dogs and that made him look for other places. Parks first and then the older part of the city, where the streets were narrow and the some had no cars at all. There were more hiding places, too, which he found useful after several men in a van tried to catch him. He was going towards them at first, wagging his tail and hoping they would be his next family, but something told him to run. Ferdie had never felt such a sense of urgency since his old owners left him by the road. Back then, he ran as fast as he could and he did exactly the same again, running away from the men in the van. The following day he wondered about that experience, especially on what caused him to feel like that. But he could never understand what it was, until one night he had a dream.

Yes, dogs have dreams. It's not just a people thing. They can also distinguish humans from … other beings. They don't call them gods, only because they have individual names for Them: there's the Silver Lady, who can shine like the full moon; the Rumbling Man, with thunder is in His voice; and Jumping Hoofs, who's occasionally spotted in the woods. There's even a god that's simply known by dogs as Ours, because He takes the canine form and so they see Him as one of them. And deities are recognizable because They're different. They shine; there's something in Their voices; and sometimes They do amazing things away from people's gaze, but not animals'. But most importantly for a dog, gods smell differently -- even when They disguise Themselves as humans. Ferdie experienced that one day at his old house, several months before his owners abandoned him. Two travellers knocked on the door, at about lunch time, and they were pilgrims on their way to a shrine on the other side of the mountains, or so they claimed. They certainly looked like the other pilgrims who used to follow the old road, but smelled differently from humans. They needed to refill their canteens and were given water. They thanked his owners and moved on, but not before one of them patted Ferdie on the head and told him they would meet again. He felt good about that and wagged his tail, if nothing else because the patting was great. A few days later, he could swear he sensed the pilgrims' smell as a thunderstorm passed over the house.

So one night, as Ferdie slept in a narrow street in Lisbon, near the monastery of Outer Saint Vincent, he dreamt of a god. He was tall and youthful, had a long cloak and wings in His shoes. He wondered if this was the Winged Guide an old dog once told him about, back when he was wandering through rural roads. And while this thought was crossing his mind, the god smiled and said: "Yes, that's me."

Ferdie actually started wagging his tail at that moment and might have woken up if the god hadn't produced a golden wand from under His cloak and waved it. He then said:

"Don't wake up yet! You need to rest for the journey ahead of you. You must follow the sun until you see the flying ram."

And then the god banged on the floor with His wand and the dream was over. Ferdie had the best night's sleep in over a year!

When he woke up, the sun was already shining high in the sky. There was a small amount of food next him, which someone had left while he was asleep. Ferdie ate it and then started thinking about his dream. He could tell that it had been more than just a dream, because he had a scent memory of it, which to him meant that the Winged Guide had really been there. So he recalled what had been told to him and looked up at the sky. The sun was already moving west and he needed to follow it. And so he did.

Ferdie took the narrow streets around the Outer Saint Vincent monastery and it didn't take him long to find himself in a great open area with a commanding view of the river. He kept going through the widest sidewalk he could find, in order to avoid the traffic and groups of both residents and tourists, but he stopped once he reached the old walls. There stood the Sun Gates, the eastern entrance of the ancient defensive line. You might think it's some great entrance, but it's really just an opening between two buildings and quite a narrow one, for that matter. It's even worse with all the cars, trams, and people moving through it, which scared Ferdie. He took a few steps back and would have run some other way, if he hadn't crashed against someone who was right behind him. He looked up and couldn't see the person's face because of the sun, but then he noticed the feet: snickers with wings! And that's when he noticed the smell and wagged his tail.

Mercury told Ferdie to follow Him and they went to an open terrace just next to the old walls, overlooking the river. They sat on the floor and talked for a while. "You need to be brave," said the god, and then He told Ferdie an old story. It was about a man named Caius Julius Catulinus, who was a priest of Octavius Augustus in the days of the Roman Empire. Born a slave, Catulinus was freed along with his parents when he was still a baby and grew up in a small house close to the theatre. One day, he had to leave the city alone to make a living elsewhere and passed through where the Sun Gates stand today. It wasn't easy: he'd never been far away from Lisbon and he would have to leave his parents, but he needed to go and so he did. It took courage to face the wide world alone and carrying little with him, but that journey opened a new life to him and he came back a wealthy and respected man -- so much so, that he ended up being chosen as a priest of Augustus and, in recognition of all that he had accomplished, he had an altar raised to Mercury close to the Sun Gates. The god then said to Ferdie:

"You need to be as brave as him! You need to cross those gates as Catulinus did and I will meet you halfway."

He stood between the arms of the Winged Guide for a while, thinking. He took a deep breath, looked at the god and then the gates, and took a few steps forward. He then stopped and looked back, only to find out that the god was gone. Ferdie sighed. He sat there for a while and then moved to the basis of a statue in front of the Sun Gates. He stayed there, watched the traffic, and when he thought things were a little quieter, he took another deep breath and carefully moved through the narrow sidewalk.

Shortly beyond the Gates, Ferdie saw a small garden to his left, which he quickly walked into. He took the opportunity to take another break to enjoy his small success and, as he did, he felt the warm sun on his fur. It felt good and he recalled the warmth he used to have with his old family. But it also reminded him that he had to look for a flying ram … whatever that meant. He looked up and around him and saw nothing of the sort and so he moved on, westwards.

The street went down the hill from that garden onwards and Ferdie kept going on the left sidewalk, which looked less crowded and not as narrow as the right one. In front of the ruins of the Roman theatre, he noticed the street took a sharp turn to the left a few metres ahead. People and traffic kept moving to and from that point and Ferdie was unsure whether he should keep going straight ahead or take a detour. He stopped, unaware that he was close to the place where Catulinus's house once stood. Immediately behind him was another street that went east and downwards, but Ferdie noticed what looked like an alley. Walking to it, he found a narrow steeped passage right behind the old cathedral. It went south, but it looked safer, and that was enough for Ferdie. It was only a small detour and then he could resume his trip westwards. And so he moved down the steps, crossed an old street, and entered another one in front him. It looked like a dead end, but it turned right and then he found an archway to his left. After crossing it he saw a garden and the river.

Ferdie resumed his westwards trip with renewed confidence. He found his way through the crowds and city streets until he came upon a park to his left, just next to the river, with a tiny beach and some nice shade. As he paused under a tree, resting, he sensed that smell again.

With his snout up and moving his head in every direction, Ferdie tried to find the Winged Guide, but He was nowhere in sight. So he decided to follow his nose, which eventually took him to the inside of a train station. There were shops, escalators, and busy crowds. And then someone stopped right in front of him, someone wearing snickers with wings. Ferdie looked up and saw a young man with a backpack and a staff. He smiled, though the face was different from the one he'd seen by the Sun Gates. The smell, however, was definitely the same! He wagged his tail and the god winked. "Follow me," he said.

Mercury led Ferdie to a line of automatic doors, which were scary, because there was hardly enough time or room for a dog to pass through them. Not to mention the security guards, who probably would not look kindly on the idea. But then the weirdest thing happened: the Winged Guide banged His staff on the floor, raising a strange and thin mist that slowly crept into the train station, and it looked like Ferdie was in a dream. People were still moving, wide awake and noisy, but at the same time it felt like they were sleeping because everything seemed … hazy. As if he had just woken up. "Don't be afraid and keep walking," said Mercury. As they moved, the automatic doors opened and then both entered a train. Ferdie was amazed that no one complained about him. After his old family abandoned him, he realized that there were a lot of places where dogs were unwelcome, sometimes violently so. That no one seemed to notice him, despite the fact that he walked right through the middle of several carriages, only reinforced the idea that it looked like people were asleep. The Winged Guide sat and Ferdie laid down under the seat. It could have been a chance to rest, if not for the fact that Ferdie was too excited about not being seen, so he took the opportunity to see what people did inside a train. "Much like cars, but with more people," he thought. And then lamented the fact that there was no open window where he could put his head out.

The train stopped twice before Mercury's feet moved. As they reached the third stop, Ferdie saw those winged snickers walking towards the door and he followed suit. As they got off at the Belém terminal, he noticed that things weren't as dream-like as before. People seemed more awake, less slow, and indeed some noticed him as he moved towards an overpass. The Winged Guide too was faster, sometimes moving like the wind, and Ferdie had a hard time keeping up. He saw the god going right on the overpass and then left towards the gardens. He was starting to get only glimpses of Him, as if Mercury was fading into the green scenery, until he finally stopped seeing Him at all. The last time Ferdie saw the Winged Guide, He was looking at him and standing next to a tree stump. Then He vanished, prompting doubt. Was this a prank? He had heard about the god's strong sense of humour and that He wasn't afraid to use it, so maybe there was a practical joke in all of this. Looking up and around, Ferdie tried to find a flying ram, but there was none to be seen. Then again, he'd never heard of such an animal. "Why didn't I think about that before," he thought. He'd crossed old Lisbon from one end to another, taken a train, rushed in the last moment, and now … now he was getting tired …. The excitement, the commotion, and even the awe had hidden a growing exhaustion. He had been walking for hours and the train ride had hardly been restful, thanks to the excitement of the whole experience. But now he had stopped and was sitting on the grass and under a warm sun, thinking on what to do next. After several minutes, he finally felt tired. Eventually, he laid down and fell asleep.

When Ferdie woke up, the sun was nearing dusk. He opened his eyes and saw an orange sky with a few clouds moving slowly. They had odd shapes and one of them looked like a ram and .... Ferdie sprang to his feet and looked up with big eyes! It was a cloud shaped like a ram! A flying ram! But as he was about to run after it, he realized he wasn't alone. There was something or someone next to him that he hadn't noticed yet. He slowly turned to his right and saw a little boy looking at him. Ferdie thought for a while. The boy obviously wasn't afraid of dogs and probably had no intention of hurting him. He could have done that while he was asleep. He gave it a try and wagged his tail and the boy smiled, stretching out an open hand with berries. Ferdie remembered eating those when he went for walks in the fields with his previous owners. The boy moved his hand towards him, as if wanting to offer him the berries. His tail wagged again and he filled his mouth with the first meal in hours! The boy laughed and gave him more food. There was instant friendship in that moment. Between them, carved on the tree stump, were the Latin words *Deo Mercurio.*

After a while, two humans showed up. They were the boy's parents and were calling him. "Time to go," the mother said. He got up and started walking away, but then heard a yelp. Looking back, he stared and then called his parents. He wanted to take Ferdie with him, but found himself having to convince Mom and Dad:

"What if he has an owner?" they asked.

"This skinny?" the boy replied. "He's obviously a stray dog." He also pointed out that Ferdie didn't have a collar and how dirty he was. And he obviously wanted to go with them. Ferdie moved closer to the boy and licked his hand. There was a moment of silence, some whispering, a bit of tail wagging and then a decision: one less stray dog on the streets!

Several months later, Ferdie went for a walk with his new owners, who decided to take an historical Sunday tour around the old city walls. As they approached the Sun Gates, there was a familiar smell in the air. Ferdie's eyes eventually found a pair of winged snickers in the crowd and he recognized Mercury. Ferdie wagged his tail. The god smiled and bowed before vanishing.

The End

* Some things in this tale are true. Lisbon's street plot is accurate and there is an 18th century reference to an altar to Mercury next to the Sun Gates. It was raised by a C. Iulius C., making Catulinus a possible last name, and the inscription also says he was an Augustal. The tree stump with the words *Deo Mercurio* is also real and it stands on the edge of a park in Belém as a modern public altar.

Hymn to Hermes and Hekate
by Rebecca Buchanan

pathfinders
they are called
and waywalkers and
keybearers and
gatekeepers
they watch over doors and
roads and
highways
every time
you walk through a door or
turn a corner or
take an off ramp
you are entering their realm
gods who can smooth your path or
trip you up with every step
      -- be nice

Hermekate's Moment
by P. Sufenas Virius Lupus

While honey-born Melikertes languished
(before he became Palaimon celebrated
in the Isthmian games at Corinth)
betwixt worlds, partially in Poseidon's
watery realm bodily; his *aion* elsewhere,
already in Helios' sphere returned;
his *thymos* circling Selene's surface;
his *nous* in ether dispersed,
his *menos* buried in Gaia's bosom,
while his *psyche* had already fled
to the fine fields of Elysium ...

Like Aktaion's flesh in hound's mouth,
Hekate, titanic overseer of everything,
mistress eternal of all ways, went
retrieving each part of the hero.
She who grants victory in horse-races
was eager to ensure the hero's restoration,
tracking him in earth, ocean, and sky.
As swift as thought arriving and departing
the divine herdsman of souls, Hermes,
gathered the scattered pieces
of the gestating god of games.

At a crossroads beneath the earth
on this side of Styx but beneath sunset
the Argus-slayer met the Zeus-beloved.
The two possessed pieces, puzzle-like,
of the mangled Meliouchos.
Quick as a whim, strong as surety,
the two travelers eyed each other

with chthonic coldness, celestial concern,
and like the hidden fires of the underworld
mutual lust seethed in their starkness
and their minds mingled without coupling.

In a moment, fully formed as Athena
from Zeus' skull, a daughter was born
to the two keepers of the crossroads.
Bright, fierce, and raging was she,
a mirror of mother and father's movements,
and yet inborn with longing
for what parents had not enjoyed.
She was called Brimo, born without birth
with a body as young and beautiful
as the fundament of the cosmos
and as complex and captivating.

Daughter desired to know her father
in much more than merely his mind;
likewise she wished to become
what her mother already was.
She voiced her requests to the pair
with speech that could not be refused.
Divine daughter double of Oedipus,
father and mother knew without oracles
that such transgressions may entail
things unforeseen even for gods,
fearful even to contemplate.

Though in agreement, they hesitated,
not knowing how to fulfill these things.
Brimo spoke, "I will see you two
become one, not as myself,
before I become she and he has me."

With no action on their parts
the two chthonic characters
moved together, merged, were remade
into a being split bilaterally
in a vertical line down the axis,
and androgyne of opposing sides.

Brimo marveled at what had never
been seen amongst mortals nor gods:
a creature neither male nor female,
not like Hermaphroditos or Agdistis,
nor even the culmination of Chaos —
and for a moment too powerful to last
lest the very form and fabric of the cosmos
cleave apart or cleave together
when lightning split sky not from Zeus
when earth shook and shattered not by Poseidon
the all-powerful Hermekate shined in glory.

Brimo's wish fulfilled, then Hermes approached,
copulated with Brimo in the blink of an eye
and went his way without Melikertes.
She who had gathered what was scattered
looked to her daughter, then became her;
and what for only a moment had been Hermekate
in shadow's obscurity also was added.
Hekate Triformis, ferocious one with six arms
called upon in spells and given suppers
resulted from that meeting at the *trivium*
when Meliouchos was made godly.

64 Adorations for Hermes
by Jennifer Lawrence

I adore you, friend of man,
I adore you, traveler and guardian of travelers,
I adore you, silver-tongued speaker,
I adore you, guide to the final destination,
I adore you, swift-footed,
I adore you, who carries the kerykeion,
I adore you, mountain-born,
I adore you, Maia's son,
I adore you, who restored Persephone to her mother's side,
I adore you, light-fingered,
I adore you, who lent pédila to Perseus,
I adore you, father of Pan,
I adore you, whom no lock may resist,
I adore you, master of ravens,
I adore you, given to playing tricks,
I adore you, who led away Apollo's cattle,
I adore you, who waits at the crossroads,
I adore you, who stands outside every door,
I adore you, whose scepter brings sleep,
I adore you, thief at the gates,
I adore you, patron of wrestlers,
I adore you, escort for the dead,
I adore you, creator of the lyre,
I adore you, who gave moly to Odysseus,
I adore you, represented by piles of stones,
I adore you, Apollo's brother,
I adore you, lucky one,
I adore you, who brings the word of Zeus to man,
I adore you, doom of Argus,
I adore you, foe of watchdogs,

I adore you, who proclaimed his own innocence,
I adore you, thoughtful one,
I adore you, who wins every race,
I adore you, most cunning,
I adore you, who knows every language,
I adore you, speaker with bees,
I adore you, deathless one,
I adore you, who receives the sacrifices of travelers,
I adore you, son of Zeus,
I adore you, who marks every boundary,
I adore you, who guided Priam to safety,
I adore you, who sang of his own cleverness,
I adore you, who watches over the markets,
I adore you, protector of shepherds,
I adore you, who bestows charm,
I adore you, arbiter and interpreter,
I adore you, great-grandfather to Odysseus,
I adore you, creator of fire,
I adore you, who enters and leaves Hades' realm at will,
I adore you, lord of Arcadia,
I adore you, who gives luck to the luckless,
I adore you, patron of public speakers,
I adore you, who excels at every contest,
I adore you, who sends prophecy in dreams,
I adore you, who turned Battos to stone,
I adore you, whose voice is echoed in the rooster's crow,
I adore you, who transformed the tortoise,
I adore you, who gifted Pandora with lies,
I adore you, who speaks in dreams,
I adore you, crafty one,
I adore you, who maps out the stars,
I adore you, wanderer along every road,
I adore you, who spoke before his first day ended,
I adore you, my lord and friend.

Arcadia
by Ariana Dawnhawk

Here it is rocky, more suitable for sheep than people
A wild place, not the refined paradise some imagine it as
Here paths trace the hills
and out of the restless winds and streams
come words, come stories
and laughter.
A scattering of pebbles
a scattering of dice
and the patterns make the next turn in the road
make the paths down into eventual darkness
and Hermes watches.

Strange Beasts
by Jason Ross Inczauskis

[*Author's Note: The following is a work of fiction. Any resemblance to other persons, animals, or events, real or imaginary, is purely coincidental. In the event that this coincidence occurs and you find it unpleasing, please accept my apologies and know that it was unwitting, and that I intended no harm.*]

It was a cold, hard winter. The freezing snow had fallen for a long time, and it was now all the way up to Clyde's shoulders. It made things harder for him. It was still loose enough that it couldn't yet hold his weight, so he was forced to push through it as best he could, occasionally shaking the cold white flakes from his coat. At least it helped protect him from the biting wind. He hadn't had a good meal in quite a while, and he had decided that if he couldn't find easy food close to his small shelter, he'd just have to brave the cold forest to search for some.

An empty stomach can be a hard master. If it hadn't been for that, Clyde might have been paying closer attention. As it was, though, he was intent on finding his meal. He pushed his way through a pile of deeper snow, far taller than he was, and then found himself out in the open. The trees still hung overhead, but there wasn't any good place to climb into them. He knew he should be careful, with no quick means of escape, but he didn't plan to be in the open long. He began to pick his way across the clearing, stepping carefully on the icy pebbles. 'Not much further,' he thought, his eyes on his destination.

Then he heard the beast. He whirled to look at it

as it raced into view. The great armored creature roared at Clyde, its gleaming eyes firmly fixed upon him. Clyde turned to run, his feet slipping over the stones in his haste, but the beast was faster than he was. The creature made an attempt to bite him, its jaws slamming into his back and sending him flying. Clyde bounced painfully along the stones before landing in a heap in the snow bank. He tried to move, but he was hurt too badly, and his legs didn't want to obey him. He cried a little, waiting for the beast to come and finish the job, but it never returned. Perhaps it had thought he'd gotten away. He lay there for awhile, feeling colder, the pain in his limbs a dull ache rather than a shooting pain. He still couldn't move, so badly had the beast's vicious attack damaged his poor body.

"Hello there," a sad voice said. Clyde tried to look at the speaker, but he was too weak at this point, and his vision was a little too blurry. "Looks like you took quite a hit. Don't worry. I'm here to help you." Clyde felt himself lifted up, as the stranger began to carry him.

"Do you have any food?" Clyde asked weakly, a little delirious from the pain.

"You will have plenty to eat very soon, Clyde. Now get some rest." He had a moment to wonder how the stranger had known his name, before he faded into painless sleep.

***

Clyde's eyes snapped open. He looked around in confusion, not recognizing the place he was in.

"It's okay, relax," the stranger's voice said. "You are safe now. There's no need to fear. I'm here to help you."

Clyde looked suspiciously at the stranger, who looked much like himself, though he wore bird's wings on his feet and on the stick that he carried. A couple small snakes curled around it, watching him. "Who are you? How did you know my name?" Clyde asked.

The stranger laughed. "I came looking for you," he said. "I was going to guide you into death, but I took pity on you, and nursed you back to health instead. It seems you were not supposed to be out wandering that night, and had had a chance for a much longer life. I am simply setting things right, really."

Clyde wasn't certain he believed him, but he decided that he wasn't going to push the issue. He was still alive, after all, and the stranger seemed to be the one responsible for that. "You didn't tell me who you are," he pointed out.

"I am called many things, in many different languages. I am the Bringer of Luck and the Giver of Good Things. To some, I am a Messenger, to others a Guide of Souls. To you, my fellow thief, I am a Friend. You may call me Hermes, if you like."

Clyde didn't think he was a thief. In fact, he never stole! Well, sometimes, when he was really hungry, or if he found something especially shiny, but other than that …. Clyde decided not to object about being called a thief, and instead asked another question. "Why do you wear bird's wings on your feet?"

"Would you believe that they make me run faster?" he suggested, grinning.

Clyde decided that he wasn't going to get a straight answer out of him unless Hermes wanted him to, so he let the subject drop. Besides, he had a more important question to ask. "Do you have any food?"

"Of course," Hermes replied, producing a shiny

foil bundle with a flourish.

Clyde's eyes went wide at the sight of it. Hermes set it down in front of him, and Clyde wasted no time tearing it open. Delicious scents assaulted his nose, and he immediately began to wolf it down as quickly as he could. After several bites, though, he paused, feeling a little guilty. Hermes was still smiling at him, watching him eat. "Would you like some?" Clyde asked. He wasn't used to sharing with anyone, but somehow it seemed appropriate.

"Why, thank you," Hermes said, reaching out and plucking up the smallest bit of food and devouring it. That seemed to be all he wanted, though, so Clyde finished it off.

"No, thank you," Clyde said gratefully. "It was delicious."

"I'm glad you liked it," he said. "I can lead you back home whenever you are ready."

Clyde was reluctant. He liked his new friend, who let him eat most of the food. He was grateful for still being alive. On top of that, he didn't think there was likely to be any more food back home now than there had been before he'd left.

"Of course," Hermes continued, "if you were looking for something more ..."

"I'd like some more," Clyde agreed eagerly. He was still a little hungry, and anything he didn't finish he could carry back with him.

"Nah, you wouldn't be interested," Hermes said.

"No, I'm interested," Clyde said. "I'm very interested."

"Well, I happen to know a place where there's all sorts of food," he replied cheerfully. Hermes hesitated briefly, before continuing. "It isn't the safest place, though. You'd need to be very brave."

"I'm brave," Clyde insisted, fearing that his new friend might not share the location of this wonderful place.

"Well, I have to warn you ... this place is loud."

"I'm not afraid of loud," Clyde said.

"There are few trees," Hermes warned.

Clyde hesitated for a moment, then decided that if there was abundant food, he could deal with the absence of a few trees. "I can manage."

"There are beasts," Hermes said. "Many beasts. More than you've ever seen. And these are strange beasts. Many different kinds. Some like the one that attacked you. Others are stranger still ...." Hermes was smiling widely.

"I'll ... I'll face the beasts," Clyde declared. "I will go to this strange place, and I will relieve the strange beasts of their food!"

"That's the spirit!" Hermes said cheerfully. "And because you have so much courage, I shall give you two very special gifts. The first gift I give to you will be very useful. Many of the beasts of this place speak strange tongues. You would not understand them, nor would they understand you. I have a talent for languages, though, and I shall share this with you. From this point on, you shall understand what they are saying as best as possible, though you shall not be able to speak to them in return." With this said, Hermes tapped Clyde lightly on the top of his head with the snake covered stick. "The second gift is far more special, though. When you are in a dire situation, call to me, and I shall come to help you once more. Be certain that it is the right time, though, because I shall only save you again once. Do you understand?"

"I do," Clyde said. "Thank you, my friend. I am grateful for everything that you have given to me."

"Good. Glad to hear it. Now, with that done, I shall take you to the place I speak of," he said. "The beasts there are not your friends, but I can see that you are a brave one, so you should be able to survive. If you are clever and quick, as well, that is. Let us be off. I hope you're not afraid of heights."

Before Clyde could answer, Hermes had scooped him up, and was bounding upwards into the sky. Clyde looked down at the ground rapidly receding below him, then up at the clouds that were coming entirely too close. Clyde decided that he'd close his eyes rather than worry about the height. He squeezed them shut, and didn't dare open them until Hermes told him that they were on the ground again.

"You can fly!" Clyde accused, nervously backing away from his friend.

"Yeah, probably should have mentioned that," he said. "Oh well, too late now. Well, here we are. Good luck to you."

Clyde looked around, and realized he was currently between two large, sheer rock faces. He tilted his head back, and determined that they had to go all the way up to the sky. He looked behind him, and noted that though the rock faces stretched high, they didn't seem to be very wide.

"Thank you …." Clyde trailed off. As he turned back around, he saw that Hermes had disappeared while he was distracted. "Guess I'm on my own, now." He looked both ways, before determining that he could probably see more of this bizarre place if he crawled out of the side of the valley that opened up into the larger area.

Clyde slowly crept to the edge of the rock face, and marveled at what he saw. There were rock faces as far as he could see on either side of the long clearing which cut between them like a river. Some of these rock faces were far taller than the ones he'd been standing between. The rock faces were riddled with caves. Soft light flowed forth from some of them, though others were dark. Some of them, especially the ones closest to him, even seemed to be covered in a thin layer of ice. Light seemed very abundant here, despite the late hour, thanks to those caves. Even some of the trees were glowing brightly.

Amazing, he thought, already beginning to wonder what sort of food would be available in a place like this. Eagerly, he walked out into the clearing, sniffing the air. He could get the occasional whiff of something delicious, though the scents passed quickly in the winter wind. He began to follow them, already feeling hungry again. Once again, though, Clyde let the thoughts of food distract him. He almost didn't see the beast, but he was fortunate. The sight of it filled him with terror, and Clyde dove for cover behind a small bush growing up against one of the rock faces. He almost called out for Hermes to save him, but resisted the urge to do so. Gradually, he worked up his courage to peek out and see if the beast was still there.

It was. In fact, it hadn't moved at all. When he realized what had happened, Clyde breathed a sigh of relief. "It's sleeping," he said quietly. He hadn't realized that the strange armored beasts would sleep standing up, but that was clearly what it was doing. Its eyes were closed, and it was breathing so faintly that Clyde couldn't even hear it. Clyde decided to sneak by it as quietly as possible, so as not to wake it.

As he walked on, Clyde could hear a faint growling sound that he knew wasn't his stomach. It was definitely coming closer, too. Clyde looked around, trying to pinpoint the source of the threatening sound, then saw the gleam of a beast's eyes up ahead. It was headed towards him quickly. With a whimper, Clyde threw himself beneath a large rock that had a small opening just large enough for him to squeeze under. It was open on all sides, as the rock was only attached to the rocks beneath it in four places, but it might give him a chance to think of a plan to escape. He was just about to call for Hermes to rescue him when the growling armored beast raced by him. Another beast, this one a bit quieter, was chasing after it, and gave no indication if it had even seen him. The first one must have been so intent on escaping its pursuer that it didn't even notice Clyde. He waited until he was certain they were both gone before venturing out into the open once more.

Clyde moved swiftly from one shadowed place to another. Hermes had definitely been right. There were many beasts here, and they seemed to enjoy sleeping out in the open. The more he walked, the more of them he saw doing so. He didn't even allow himself to breathe as he passed by a valley between two of the rock faces that seemed to contain an entire nest full of them. They slept in rows beside each other, and he silently prayed that they would not awaken. As the brilliant eyes of one of them flashed open with a growl, he ran. Clyde was certain that the one beast would awaken the others, and he was almost ready to call Hermes to his rescue when he looked back, and saw the beast was now running in the opposite direction. He breathed a quick sigh of relief, but wasted no time putting some more distance between himself and that nest of beasts.

It wasn't long, though, before he found another one. All of these beasts seemed to be asleep, and none of them stirred as he went by. *I see how it is,* Clyde marveled silently to himself. *The beasts sleep very deeply. The one that woke up hadn't noticed me. It had something it needed to do. If they sleep so deeply, then I just need to watch out for the ones that are waking up!* With this thought, Clyde was feeling a little better. He realized that he could find a good place to hide during the day, and come out to get food after the beasts went to sleep again. It wouldn't even necessarily be that hard to find a place to hide, as the spaces between some of the rock faces looked like they might be too small for the beasts to fit into.

As he walked, he found that one of these spaces actually smelled of food. *Oh, this is too perfect,* he thought. *Too small for beasts, and filled with food!* He quickly ran into the space, trampling over the piles of junk that littered the area as he did so. One of these, a pile of clothes, suddenly moved as ran over it. Clyde pressed himself against the rock face, trembling in fear.

"Who's there?!" a strange voice bellowed, as the pile of clothes moved to reveal a new type of beast that had been wrapped in them. The beast was much larger than Clyde, though not nearly so large as the armored ones that roamed the open areas. This beast had scraggly fur covering its face, some hanging down from its lower jaws. The beast was grimy, as though it hadn't groomed itself in quite awhile. The smell from it confirmed that fact. It looked one way, then another, its eyes eventually settling on Clyde, who by this point was about to call Hermes to his aid. The beast sighed. "You scared me," it grumbled, wrapping the clothes around itself and settling back into its original position. "It's too cold out for this," it grumbled quietly.

So that's what Hermes was talking about when he mentioned the beasts that spoke in a strange tongue, Clyde thought, calming down as the beast went back to sleep. It seemed that the one he'd disturbed had been too busy sleeping to bother with him, but now that he knew what they were like, he knew he needed to be more cautious, even in the smaller areas. Those beasts could be anywhere. Clyde slowly moved away from the rock face, and hurried away from the beast, which now growled in its sleep. He didn't want to be there when the beast woke up again.

As Clyde walked on, the smell of food continued to draw him onwards. Hermes had been right. There was much food present in this place. He still had not managed to find any for himself, though. He hoped that the smell would lead him to some that was not guarded by any beasts. He was overjoyed when he spotted the great green rock. The food smell was coming from within. Clyde began to walk around the outside of it, his joy diminishing considerably. The rock was far taller than he was, and there didn't seem to be any way to get at the food that was inside of it. He pressed himself to the ground, and crawled beneath it to look for any holes that might lead into it. Eventually, he acknowledged that the hole containing the food must be on the top of the rock. Clyde moved behind the rock, and started trying to scale it.

Clyde soon determined that the rock was too smooth to climb, but that by pressing his back against the green rock, he could climb the rougher rock face to make progress. He was about halfway to the top when a loud crash from above caused him to drop back to the ground in fear. Clyde ran out from the behind the green rock, quickly trying to find both a place to hide and the source of the crash.

A strange beast, much like the one he'd so recently awoken, was standing in front of the green rock. This beast, too, was wrapped in rags, and stood upon only half of its legs. It had first been reaching into the rock, but now the beast was watching Clyde. "Oh, hey there, little guy," the beast said. "I didn't mean to scare you. It's okay, I won't hurt you. You want some food?"

Clyde couldn't believe his luck. *This beast isn't dangerous*, he thought. *He doesn't want to hurt me or eat me. He wants to give me food!* Clyde walked forward, still a little nervous, but the excitement was beginning to build within him.

"Here you go, little guy," the beast said. "Some for you, some for me. A good meal for both of us." The beast pulled something out of the rock, which he had apparently opened by pulling up some sort of flap resting on top of it. He broke it into two pieces, then tossed one down to the ground by Clyde.

No wonder I couldn't find the food, Clyde thought. *It was covered up in there.* He walked over to what had been dropped and picked it up. It had different textures to it. The top of it was soft, and covered in small seeds. The bottom was wet and gooey. In between, there was some sort of meat, as well as a leaf and other things that Clyde could not identify. All of them smelled delicious, though, and he wasted no time eating what the strange beast had decided to share.

"Pretty good, huh?" the beast asked. Clyde agreed, but he couldn't really tell the beast that.

Their meal was interrupted as light poured forth from a cave with a crash. A beast stood there, growling with rage at the two of them. This beast was tall and thin, though still clearly of the same type as the friendly beast who gave Clyde food. This one lacked much fur, though it had a long mane of it flowing down its back. The beast shivered, and Clyde could not tell whether it was trembling in rage or shivering from the cold.

"Get out of here!" the beast yelled. "There's nothing for you here!"

Clyde began to run away as quickly as his legs could carry him, thinking briefly that he should call to Hermes to save him. He probably would have, but it didn't take him long to realize that the other beast was apparently standing its ground, and yelling back at the one that had interfered with their meal. The beast yelled that the food was perfectly good, and that it wasn't right that it should go to waste when there were those who needed it.

Clyde thought to himself as he ran, *If I could be heard by the beasts, I would go and stand beside the friendly one that gave me food. We would yell at that angry beast, and chase it away together, so that we could keep that food and not let it go to waste. I would be brave enough to do so.* But of course, Clyde was not able to make himself understood. Hermes had not given him that particular gift, so as brave as Clyde might be, running was all he could think to do.

He ran until he began to run out of breath, trying his best to avoid those large open areas that were prowled by the great armored beasts with fierce gleaming eyes. When he could run no further, Clyde stopped, and tried to catch his breath. He heard no sounds of pursuit, but he did hear a distant rumble, as well as some strange, screeching sounds which he could not begin to describe. *That must be yet another beast*, Clyde thought. It sounded like a large one, so he hoped that he was in an area that was too small for it to enter.

As his heart rate began to settle, and his breath returned to him, Clyde became aware of an enticing scent. *Food,* Clyde thought. *That's food, and a lot of it!* Clyde hurried off to find the source of the scent, and it didn't take him long to do so. It was another smooth green rock, much like the one that the friendly beast had pulled the food from. This one was even better, though. The flaps that were used to cover the top were already open, as there was too much in the hollow of the rock for them to lay flat.

I have found the perfect rock! Clyde thought excitedly. He briefly considered going and finding the friendly beast to show him this one, but realized that he could no longer remember exactly where it had been. *Hopefully, the friendly beast will smell this food and come here on its own. If not, then there is simply more for me.* With that thought, Clyde leapt at the rock, eventually managing to get a good enough grip that he could climb up into it.

The scents within were almost overpowering. There were so many of them, each of them different, all of them potent. Clyde walked along the soft bundles, taking them all in. It seemed as though the food was wrapped in bundles, covered by thin black film. This film proved quite easy to tear apart, though, and Clyde was soon feeling around inside them, finding the bits of food that had been stored within. *There is enough food here, I don't ever need to leave!* Clyde thought excitedly, as he began to eat.

Clyde was so intent on his meal, that he almost didn't notice the danger approaching. If the beast had not been so loud, it likely would have caught him snacking, completely unprepared for it. The beast was quite loud, however, and Clyde was quickly alerted to its approach. Clyde looked up, and beheld the largest armored beast he had ever seen. Clyde dropped the food he was holding, and tried to hide behind one of the black bundles containing the food. He was so terrified, that he dared not call for Hermes yet, lest it draw the beast's attention to him.

The beast, growling loudly, moved past the rock, and for a second, Clyde thought that perhaps it was after something else entirely. This hope was quickly squashed, though, as the beast suddenly stopped. It began to back towards the rock, letting out the bizarre screeching noises that Clyde had heard just a little while before. Up close, they were even louder and more terrifying to him. Clyde froze where he was, trembling in fear. He held his breath, for fear that the beast might hear it and turn around.

Then he watched as one of the smaller beasts climbed off of it. The beast walked towards the rock, standing on only half of its legs. Clyde watched it, not moving. Then, the beast crouched down, and began to move the entire rock. Clyde fell backwards at the sudden movement, but quickly righted himself.

As he peered over the side of the rock, he realized that it was being lifted by the armored beast. It had reached behind itself, and was now lifting the entire thing! Clyde watched in horror as he realized that it was about to pour the entire contents of the rock into a great maw in the beast's back. As the bundles of food began to shift beneath him, moving inevitably towards the waiting maw, Clyde leapt.

He tried to catch himself on the beast, but the armor provided no purchase, and he tumbled to the rocks below. The smaller beast yelped in shock when Clyde crashed down in front of it, but Clyde wasted no time in running. Silently, he prayed that the armored beast would be too busy devouring the food from the rock to give chase.

Once more, Clyde ran until he could go no further. He collapsed in a pile beside a large rock, gasping for breath and trembling with weakness. *I survived*, he marveled silently to himself. *I faced a great beast, and survived.* If he had not been so weak, he would have been excited at that thought, but at this point, he desperately needed to rest.

Clyde laid there for what seemed to him to be hours, though what was likely only a few minutes in reality. His breath gradually returned to him, though the weakness in his limbs remained. His stomach rumbled, demanding immediate satisfaction. *So much lost food ...,* Clyde thought, sadly remembering each interrupted meal. He laid there, his hunger and exhaustion warring within him. Exhaustion almost won, and would have, if not for the faint hint of a delicious smell carried on the wind.

Clyde pushed himself to his feet. *I can't give up*, he thought, courage rising up within him. *There is food in this strange place, and I'm going to find it. I have faced the strange beasts, and I have survived. I am tired, bruised, and hungry, but I'm alive!* His heart filled with a sense of confidence that he had never known before.

He set out to find the food he smelled. The scent grew stronger the closer he got to it. When he found the source, he was surprised to find that this food was trapped in a rock. The rock was so full of holes that it was more hole than rock. Clyde reached through one of the holes, stretching for the food, but no matter how much he strained, Clyde could not grasp the food within. Clyde sat back to consider this. *The food in there is too far away to reach, and too large to have just slipped through one of the holes. There must be a larger hole somewhere that allowed it in.*

Clyde began to walk around the stone, soon noticing that there was a larger opening, but that there was a solid barrier blocking off the food within it. Tentatively, Clyde pushed the barrier, and was surprised to find that it bent inwards, opening a route to the food. *I was right,* he thought excitedly. *This is a flap like the ones covering the larger food rocks. I can open this one, though.* Clyde rushed in, and began to eat the food. It was enough that he soon did not feel even the slightest bit hungry.

That was a good meal, he thought happily, turning to crawl back out of the rock. He felt his heart sink as he realized that the flap had closed behind him. A feeling of panic began to rise within him when he realized that it couldn't be pushed from this side, and he had no way to get a grip on it to pull it open. "I'm trapped…," he said softly, trying to push his fear down long enough to figure out a way to escape.

A flash of light caused him to freeze in his struggles. A great armored beast was heading straight towards him. The beast stopped close by, and two of the smaller beasts climbed off of it. "No, no, no!" Clyde wailed. 'They're going to feed me to the beast!' The thought filled him with terror, and he began to throw himself at the sides of the rock, hoping a weak point might break and give him his freedom.

"Got another one," one of the beasts said. "Look at him fight."

"He's a spirited one, I'll give him that," the other said, bending down and lifting up the rock that was now Clyde's prison.

They walked behind the great armored beast, and opened up a maw on the back of it. Clyde screamed as they prepared to toss his rock into it. "Hermes! Help me, now, Hermes! Save me!" Clyde desperately cried.

"Loud little guy, ain't he?" the beast carrying him said, tossing him into the armored beast's maw.

"Sure is," the other one replied as the armored beast's maw closed, leaving Clyde in complete darkness.

Clyde could hear rumbling as the beast began to move once more. He paced back and forth within the rock. He was still alive, but still trapped. *Why hasn't Hermes saved me? I called to him, and he didn't save me. Was it too dangerous for him? Is there something wrong with me?* He continued to pace and worry like this until the beast stopped again, this time, the rumblings within quieting as well.

The beast's mouth opened once more, and the one that had thrown him into it reached in and pulled it out again. Clyde began to struggle once more, but he couldn't manage to break out of the rock. "Easy, boy," the beast said. "Everything's going to be alright."

Easy for you to say, Clyde thought to himself. Apparently, this beast knew that he could understand them, and was trying to get him to make it easy on them. Clyde would not be that cooperative. He threw himself with all of his might at the side of the rock, and it caused the beast to stumble.

"Calm down!" the beast said, now clearly growing angry. "Let's get this one in a cage, quick."

The two smaller beasts walked into one of the brightly lit caves, leaving the armored one outside. They walked through several chambers, each one sterile and quiet. This cave did not seem lived in, despite the presence of the beasts within. The last chamber, though, housed their prison. Creatures of numerous shapes and sizes struggled against the bars of cages, calling for help and freedom that these beasts would not give to them. The beasts placed the rock against one of the cages, pulled up the flap, and forced Clyde into it, then walked away, leaving him alone with the other creatures.

At first, Clyde didn't even look around. He could smell food nearby within his cage, but it smelled like it would not be very tasty, and he had already eaten anyway. Eventually, though, he looked up, and began to stare around the chamber, at the other prisoners. He was shocked when he realized that the cage beside him contained one like him, but this one was female. A very beautiful female, with an alluring scent …. Clyde caught himself staring, and quickly tried to look away. Soon, though, he was looking at her once more.

"Hello," he said quietly. "My name is Clyde. What's yours?"

"Claudia," she said. "How did these monsters catch you?"

"I got stuck in a rock while trying to get some food," he said. "You?"

"Me, too," she said sadly.

"I like you," Clyde said. "I like you a lot. I wish we had met under better circumstances."

"I like you, too," Claudia said. "It is too bad that we're doomed."

Maybe they don't want to hurt us …. Clyde thought. He didn't really believe it, but he now hoped that maybe the beast had been truthful when it said that everything would be alright. It didn't seem right that he would meet Claudia like this, only to have her snatched away.

"Yes, they do," she said. "I've been here for a little while now. A lot of things come in. A lot of things go back out. But once they take someone away, they never come back."

Clyde gulped. "Maybe we have hope," he said. "I have a friend. He may rescue us. His name is Hermes. Have you met him?"

"I have not," she said. "He'd best hurry, though, if he's going to."

At that moment, a different beast walked in. This one had a long mane of fur as well, and Clyde quickly rushed to the back of the cage to get as far away as possible. The beast, though, didn't look at him. It bent down, and pulled out a cage containing a four legged creature with a long, skinny tail.

Claudia began to pace back and forth rapidly, trying to find some way out, but the beast just bared its teeth at her, and said, "Don't worry. Your turn's next." With that said, the beast turned and left, carrying the other creature with her.

"We need to get you out of here!" Clyde exclaimed. "It just said that you're next!"

Claudia's eyes went wide. "It did?! You can understand them? I'm next?!" At this, she began to fling herself desperately at the bars of her cage.

"Hermes!" Clyde screamed out, sorrow in his voice. "Please come and help! Even if you won't help me, please help her!" The other creatures stared at him, but Clyde didn't care. He continued calling for Hermes, until his lungs were raw and his spirits the lowest they had ever been. Despair filled him, and he sank down, whimpering, to the floor of his cage.

The entryway to the chamber creaked open, and one of the beasts walked into the room. Clyde looked up at them, wishing that he could beg them to take him instead, but something was different about this one.

94

Though it walked on only half of its legs like the other beasts, and indeed seemed to be one of them, it wore bird's wings on its feet and on the stick with snakes that it carried.

"Hello, Clyde," the beast said.

"Hermes?" Clyde asked in disbelief. "You look like a strange beast, now!"

"I can look many different ways," he said with a chuckle.

"Why didn't you come to save me?" he asked.

"I did come to save you," Hermes replied. "I'm right here, aren't I?"

Clyde looked down. "I'm sorry, I've just been so panicked .... Forget me," he said, looking back at Hermes. "Please, save Claudia. Get her to safety."

Hermes laughed. "Clyde, I am here to save both of you. Would you like to come out of that cage, now?"

"Yes, please, thank you," Clyde said. Hermes tapped the cage with his stick, and it popped open to allow Clyde to exit. He repeated the process with Claudia's cage.

"Thank you, Hermes, sir," she said quietly, climbing out to join Clyde.

"Here's my recommendation," Hermes said, tapping on the side of the cave wall, causing an opening to appear. "You two should climb through this tunnel, head to the left, and keep going until you smell fresh air. I'll meet you outside."

"What are you going to do?" Clyde asked.

Hermes grinned. "I'm going to give them something to keep them occupied while you two make your escape." With that, he began tapping other cages, causing them to open up. Then he vanished, as though he hadn't even been there.

As the other creatures began to crawl out of their cages, Clyde helped Claudia into the small tunnel. He was about to follow, when he heard the entryway open once more.

"Oh my God!" the beast screamed. "Larry! Tim! Get in here! The animals have escaped!"

Clyde turned, and leapt for the tunnel entrance.

"There's a raccoon in the vents!" the beast shrieked, but Clyde wasn't wasting any more time. He hurried after Claudia, and soon the two of them could smell the fresh air, the promising scent of freedom drawing them towards the end of the tunnel.

Hermes was true to his word, and was waiting just at the end of the tunnel. He reached for the two of them, and soon he was flying off with them under his arms.

"He can fly!" Claudia screamed.

"Yeah," Clyde said, his eyes tightly closed. "I should have mentioned that. You might want to close your eyes."

Hermes eventually settled down in a beautiful place filled with trees and snow, though the rock faces seemed to surround the place on all sides. Still, it seemed peaceful and welcoming to the two of them. "Here you go," he said, setting them down on a branch.

"Thank you, Hermes," Clyde said. "We appreciate it."

Hermes smiled at the two of them. "You are welcome. I hope you will find this place to be a good home. It has trees for you, and is quite comfortable during the spring and summer, yet is still close enough to the city that you can go and forage for food there, if you wish. Just watch out for the cars."

"I don't understand," Clyde said. "What are the

cars?"

"They are big, and armored, and have gleaming eyes. You know them when you see them."

"Oh, yeah, I know those beasts," Clyde said.

"Well, they shouldn't be much of a problem for you here," Hermes said. "You just need to watch out when you go into the city."

"Thanks for the warning," Clyde said. "And for everything, else, too," he quickly added. Claudia echoed his sentiments.

"You are welcome," Hermes said, cheerfully stepping up into the air.

"Wait, don't go!" Clyde said, hurrying towards the end of the branch to get closer to him.

"Clyde, I cannot live here with you in this park," he said, smiling warmly at the raccoon.

"But ...." Clyde began.

"Clyde, I am a very busy god. As much as I adore the company of you and your future mate, I cannot settle down and stay with you here."

"I understand," Clyde said. "Will I ever see you again?"

"Of course you will. You will see me when you die."

"Oh ...." Clyde hung his head, disappointed.

"Don't worry," Hermes said, laughing a little. "I will still be here with you. You just won't see me. That doesn't mean I'm not still watching over you."

"But how can you be watching over me if you're not here?" Clyde asked.

"Clyde, I may not be living with you, but I am a god. I can be present without being noticed, and I can guide you without being obvious. If I lived here, you would want me to help you with everything. You would not be able to make your own decisions or have your own experiences. I would not deprive you of that. So, I shall allow you to have your experiences, and we can talk about them when you die."

Clyde looked up, a touch of humor creeping into his voice. "I guess that means that I don't want to see you again for a long time ...."

"That's the spirit!" Hermes said, starting to run off once more.

"Wait!" Clyde said again. "What do we do now?"

Hermes laughed again. "Clyde, my dear friend, isn't it obvious? Live! Go forth and have whatever adventures await you. Try new things. Take risks! Have children, and raise them to be as brave and as clever as you are. Most of all, live life! Enjoy it while it lasts. Death is not the end, but it is another journey, and it is good to have many stories to tell along the way! So go, Clyde. Take Claudia, create a wonderful life for yourselves, and live!"

"Thank you," Clyde said. "I will try to do so."

"Good," Hermes said. "I expect good things from you two." He turned and began to fly away, then paused and looked back. "Swipe some good things for me," he said with a wink, then lifted upwards into the sky.

The two raccoons drew closer together, and watched the departing god, silently sharing their company with each other. They looked out over their new home, feeling the promise of the future. Their hopes and dreams filled them with joy, and they watched in wonder as Hermes vanished into the rising sun.

Hermes Propylaios
by P. Sufenas Virius Lupus

watching them going crossing
over and back out again
i stand silent witness
guardian and support
lintel of every doorway

"one who is not an initiate"
outside of the mysteries
because for me there is no
beginning or introduction
or going in and seeing

no phallus on this herm
as sign of protection
priapic apotropaic
for it is a root a seed
a start but i have none

"know thyself" i say
advising by word and form
for those who know how
to interpret these things
for this is what i am

the interpreter mediator
translator metaphor
the most basic medium
of thought mind word
symbol sign sense

there is no me apart from
these things nor is there
a you outside or inside
of these things identity
is but a whisper on wind

of moving vibratory particles
in a vast space empty
only known because it moves
carrying point to point
the message of movement

a dance only seen
from a distance that sees
what sign symbol sense
can create what means
meaning again is "a way

or manner by which events
happen" thus not a thing
with independent essence
but again a dance
a way of moving

and what am i but
the movement the moment
static or dynamic
the particle the pattern
the ripples outward

from first forms of chaos
so all coming and going
is me and even you
have been in the chain
of being since before being

and knowing yourself
consists in nothing more
than seeing the moment
but not mistaking it
for the spaces in between

Hermes Thank You -- 3/9/07
by Ariana Dawnhawk

Running through the gateways
Running along the borders, you are
Sideways and speaking and hopeful, you are
Boundary and transgressor, merchant and thief
Clever one, swift one, true guide –
Be praised!

Prayer to Hermes
for Help Regarding Technological Difficulties
by D.L. Wood

To Hermes I pray,
I offer You these words,
Great God of Communication,
I ask You for expedient help,
Regarding my technological difficulties.
I thank You so much for being by my side,
Thank You Great Hermes,
Of Winged Foot and Cap

Prayer to Hermes I
by Rebecca Buchanan

Hermes the Honey-Tongued
Hermes the Shit-Tongued
Prince of Lies
    Sweet lies
    Putrid lies
Hermes
Double-Tongued

    -- here, a blade
    -- teach me your skill

Prayer to Hermes II
by Rebecca Buchanan

Hermes
Wayfarer
Traveler's God
Guide me safely on my journey
    and back home again

Khthonic Hermes -- The Magician
by Amanda Sioux Blake

[Note: excepted from the author's forthcoming work, *Journey to Olympos: A Modern Spiritual Odyssey*]

Hermes, I call, whom fate decrees
to dwell near to Kokytos, the famed stream of Haides,
and in necessity's *[ananke's]* dread path,
whose bourn to none
that reach it ever permits return.
O Bakkheios Hermes, progeny divine
of Dionysos, parent of the vine,
and of celestial Aphrodite, Paphian queen,
dark-eyelashed Goddess, of a lovely mien:
who constant wanderest through the sacred seats
where Haides' dread empress, Persephone, retreats;
to wretched souls the leader of the way,
when fate decrees, to regions void of day.
Thine is the wand which causes sleep to fly,
or lulls to slumberous rest the weary eye;
for Persephone, through Tartaros dark and wide,
gave thee for ever flowing souls to guide.
Come, blessed power, the sacrifice attend,
and grant thy mystics' works a happy end.
    -- *Orphic Hymn 57* to Khthonian Hermes

Many-faceted Hermes is more than the celestial Messenger of the Gods or the rural protector of flocks and shepherds. Hermes, the Guide of the Dead, assisted Herakles in his labors, showing him where the entrances to the Underworld were.(1) He also guided Persephone

106

out of the Underworld every spring when it was time for Her to rejoin Her mother.

When in the Underworld, Hermes becomes more the Guide of the Dead – He also becomes Hermes Hypnos, Lord of Dreams. The thousand Oneiroi, the Dream Gods, follow Him to the mortal world and to the sleeping men and women in it.

Hermes the Magician stands out amongst His many jobs and aspects. The Greek word for witchcraft, *pharmakia*, is the origin of our word 'pharmacy'. Indeed the art of magic and the art of herb-lore were closely related, both in reality and in myth. In *The Iliad*, the sorceress Kirke (Circe) turns Odysseus's men into swine by use of a potion, and it is an (imaginary) herb called *moly*, given to the hero by Hermes, that protects Odysseus from that same fate.(2) The use of plants, herbs, and roots could be called a medicinal practice, which is partially correct. Magic is notoriously hard to define, but herb-lore begins to overlap with magical practice when the person who harvests the plant says a prayer or recites an incantation while cutting the plant, a well-documented practice in ancient times. John Scarborough, in his essay *The Pharmacology of Sacred Plants, Herbs, and Roots*, quotes one such spell to be spoken while picking a plant before sunrise:

> I am picking you, such and such a plant, with my five-fingered hand, I,[magician's name], and I am bringing you home so that you may work for me for a certain purpose, I adjure you by the undefiled name of the god: if you pay no heed to me, the earth which produced you will no longer be watered as far as you are concerned – ever in life again, if I fail in this

operation [then follow the magical words]; fulfill for
me this perfect charm.(3)

Much of our information about Greek magic
comes from what is known as the *Papyri Graecae Magicae,*
or the *Greek Magical Papyri.* The *PGM* refers to a collection
of spells and incantations from Alexandrian Egypt. The
spells are syncretic in nature, invoking Greek and
Egyptian deities side by side. In Alexandrian Egypt,
Greeks, Egyptians, and even Jews had lived together for
generations, and the culture and religions of both lands
had blended to create a unique synthesis. The *PGM* are
an excellent source material. There are even several spells
with Jewish elements, invoking Yahweh, or Iao as He is
called in Greek. When we are raised with the modern
concept of absolute monotheism, this fact can be hard to
reconcile, even to Pagans. But it was pretty common to
the worldview of ancient polytheism to incorporate the
Gods of other lands into your worship, especially when
you were visiting or living in a land that was not your
native home.

Although many Deities of both Greek and
Egyptian origin were invoked in ancient spells and
curses, the two Gods most often associated with magic in
the Greek mind were Hermes and Hekate. Hekate is a
very complex Goddess, much more then just a Goddess
of magic, but by Roman times Her magical aspects had
swallowed up the other sides to Her, and She became the
witches' Goddess that we know today. Hermes
Trismegestos, the "Thrice-Greatest", evolved to become a
God of alchemy during the Renaissance.

It is appropriate that Hermes and Hekate have a
close relationship. It's said that an Underworld Goddess

by the name of Brimo gave Her virginity to Hermes, sleeping with Him on the banks of the Lake Boibeis in Thessaly.(4) Brimo, meaning "Angry" or "Terrifying", was an epithet of Hekate. It was also a title of both Demeter and Persephone. In this case Demeter is an unlikely interpretation. Persephone would perhaps have been justifiable, if the text in question had not said that this Brimo had been a virgin when She lay with Hermes.

In myth there were tales of Hermes, on certain occasions, leading the souls of the dead into the upper world for a short time. Laodameia was the wife of Protesilaos, the first man to die at the Trojan War. She mourned her husband greatly, and crying for hours, she prayed to be able to speak to him one last time. Hermes, with Zeus's permission, guided the soul of Protesilaos back to the earth so that he and his wife could have one last visit, and say goodbye.(5) Thus Hermes was a Deity to Whom one would appeal in the practice of necromancy, the summoning of the souls of the dead.

The modern era has inherited the medieval witch-hunter's distrust of folk magic, although most today would label it superstitious instead of evil. But in the ancient world it was not the practice itself, but the aim or goal that was looked at to determine whether it was 'good' or 'bad'.

Consultation with spirits did not have the stigma attached to it that it does today. Every person was said to have their own *Agathos Daimon*, or "Good Spirit", that protected and guided them. The Agathos Daimon fulfilled the function of what many today would call a guardian angel. Socrates said he was in constant communication with his daimon, so much so that when he went walking and came to a bend in the road his daimon told him which path he should take.

A form of ancient magic that we do not necessarily want to reproduce are curse tablets. A curse tablet was typically made of lead, and the plea was carved into the surface of the lead and then cast into a well or other body of water. There is a chilling, and fairly accurate, scene in the fifth episode of the HBO TV series *Rome* in which Servila, angry that Caesar has scorned her, curses him using one such lead tablet. Despite their sinister nature, these tablets have proven invaluable to archaeologists, giving us much information about the practice of magic and the Gods invoked in spells in ancient times.

Ginnete Paris, the author of *Pagan Grace: Dionysos, Hermes and Goddess Memory in Daily Life*, emphasizes the symbolic nature of Hermes' magic in myth, "binding and unbinding, tying and untying, attaching and detaching." (6) Apollo tries to tie Hermes up after He steals the Sun-God's cattle, but the ropes simply fall off, refusing to tie. Interestingly, the Greek word for amulet means "to bind" or "to attach". The scholar Roy Kotansky theorizes that this is because the amulet would be bound or attached to a person. (7) Katonsky goes on to explain the use of amulets in medicine, using an example from *The Odyssey*. Odysseus is wounded by a boar, and when the wound is cleaned and bound, a talisman is placed in the bandages to promote healing and stave off infection. (8)

Paris, a Jungian psychologist, is more interested in a symbolic interpretation of the myths in modern times then in ancient practice.

> It's easy to make a psychological connection between emotional situations and words like weaving, knotting, braiding, twisting, binding. The sorcerer, the therapist, the shaman and the healer are all caught up in a form

of magic in which Hermes appears,making and unmaking emotional connections, tying and untying psychological knots. ...
Secondly, language itself reflects a symbolic level of meaning in many expressions about binding: one is"bound" by a promise, "hooked" by love, "attached" to a child, "held back" by fear, or one's attention is "riveted" on something important .... Death is our "undoing", we "tie the knot" when we marry, we "break up" when we divorce ... (9)

She also connects the magic of binding with seduction, as we have seen already, as seduction creates an attraction,which Paris calls a tie holding one person to another. Hermes, as a rural God, was also invoked for fertility, for both people and flocks and herds.

The magic of Hermes is powerful and varied, used in sex and fertility, persuasion, protection of herds and flocks, necromancy and spirit-work, divination, dreams and sleep, commerce, and thievery and protection from it. He is truly a complicated God!

Notes

1) Homer. Odyssey 11.626
2) Homer. Odyssey X. 305-317
3) Papyri Graecae Magicae, as quoted by John Scarbough, *The Pharmacology of Sacred Plants, Herbs, and Roots in Magika Hiera : Ancient Greek Magic and Religion*. Edited by Christopher A. Faraone and Dirk Obbink. Oxford University Press. New York. 1991. pg 157.
4) Propertius. *Elegies* 2.29C
5) Apollodorus. *The Library* E3.30, Hyginus. Fabulae 103

6) Ginette Paris. *Pagan Grace : Dionysos, Hermes, and Goddess Memory in Daily Life.* Spring Publications. Putnam, Connecticut. pg 105

7) Roy Kotansky. *Incantations and Prayers for Salvation on Inscribed Greek Amulets, in Magika Hiera : Ancient Greek Magic and Religion.* Edited by Christopher A. Faraone and Dirk Obbink. Oxford University Press. New York. 1991. pg 107.

8) Homer. Odyssey. 19. 457-59

9) Ginette Paris. *Pagan Grace : Dionysos, Hermes, and Goddess Memory in Daily Life.* Spring Publications. Putnam, Connecticut. Pg 105 – 106

All Your Faces
by Jennifer Lawrence

(Written while contemplating becoming Exegetai of Hermes.)

I see you:

Cirque du Soleil acrobat, circus aerialist,
Windriding rope-spinner, sexy-sleek and infinitely nimble.
Springing in wild backward flips from one end of the mat to the other.
Would that I could partake of one-hundredth such grace.

Hitchhiker, forever-wanderer,
Thumb cocked backward over your shoulder,
Pointing to where you've been as you gaze
Forward to where you're headed.

Craps-shooter, wheel-turner, card shark,
Swift-breathed with excitement,
Dogs and horses both favor you
As you ride that hot, sharp, slick streak of luck
Toward the home stretch.

Sign in hand, you guide the little ones
Safely across the street.
Old woman or young man,
Protecting the children in all their potential,
Mindful of what they may someday become.

You look out of the mailman's eyes, and sail the 'netted seas;

Reporter, package-bearer, gossip at the neighborhood fence —
Each message that comes and goes bears your invisible stamp.

Wry-smiling storysmith, weaving each tale,
The lines your warp and weft.
You teach me how to share what I dream,
Making those worlds real with words.

And there, at the end, as I lay with
Eyes closed and weighted down with coin,
You wait, hand outstretched, to take me on one last journey.
With you as companion down into the depths of Hades,
I shall not fear.

Enodios, Eriounious, Kourotrophis, Diaktoros,
Logios and Charidotes, Eragonios, Psychopompos.
Your names, your faces. Someday I may know them all.

Gods and Planets:
Hermes and Mercury in Archetypal Astrology
by K.S. Roy

"I sing of Hermes... luck-bringing messenger of the
deathless gods."
-- Homeric Hymn 18 to Hermes

"Many people... resorted to the temple of Hermes
asking for the gift of wisdom... Now when on the
appointed day they arrived for the distribution of the
gifts of wisdom, Hermes as the god of wisdom and
eloquence and also of rewards, said to [he who had
presented the god with the third largest offering:]...
'You shall have the gifts of astronomy.'"
-- Philostratus, Life of Apollonius of Tyana 5. 15 (trans.
Conybeare)

To the ancients, astrology and astronomy were
two sides of the same coin, a coin held in the hand of
Hermes, to whom they credited the invention of
astronomy and the calendar. While there were -- and still
are today -- many different traditions and philosophies of
astrological practice, it remains obvious that ancient
astrologers identified the planets with their gods through
their names, and populated the starry heavens with their
myths in the form of the constellations we still recognize
today. To what degree the myths influenced astrological
symbolism has been widely debated, past and present.
My intention here is not to put that debate to rest, but
rather to explore some of the many connections between
the god Hermes and the planet Mercury in astrology.

In my own astrological philosophy, the planets

and other celestial bodies are identified with the gods through archetypal synchronicity. As Plato said in the Republic, "Perhaps there is a pattern set up in the heavens for one who desires to see it, and having seen it, to find one in himself." Archetypal astrology views the planets as archetypal symbols, whose movements correspond with the themes that play out in our own day to day lives. In this view, the planets are not causing anything to happen, but rather acting as a "synchronicity clock" of the cosmos. A clock striking noon does not make one eat lunch, but it makes it much more likely if that is the schedule you are on. Astrology shows us what schedule we're on, letting us see our lives through the perspective of planetary cycles set in motion at our birth, showing us when certain themes will be highlighted and activated throughout our lives. When looking towards the future, we can look at the archetypal themes represented by the planets and other celestial bodies to show us the best times to begin certain activities, as well as how we can best interact with the themes already in play at a given moment.

Although the planets are seen as archetypes in astrology, for most of us with Pagan or Polytheistic beliefs, the gods represented by these celestial objects are not. While I see the planets and other celestial bodies as archetypes carrying the symbolism of the gods, by no means am I reducing the gods themselves to mere archetypes. To me, the planets are archetypes, but the gods are divine. In my personal opinion, the planetary archetypes derive their meanings from the god or gods they are associated with, and by understanding these archetypal themes we can not only understand ourselves better, but come to a deeper understanding of and connection to our gods as well. In this sense, astrology

116

becomes a sacred language for understanding ourselves and our place within the cosmos.

In the language of astrology, just as Hermes is the messenger of the gods, so is Mercury considered the messenger planet. Mercury symbolizes our patterns of thought and speech, our style of communication, the way we learn and process information, as well as how we share it. Hermes is often credited for the invention of writing, language and speech, all the many ways in which we communicate with each other.

"Sokrates: Let us inquire what thought men had in giving them [the gods] their names... The first men who gave names [to the gods] were no ordinary persons, but high thinkers and great talkers... This name 'Hermes' seems to me to have to do with speech; he is an interpreter (hêrmêneus) and a messenger, is wily and deceptive in speech, and is oratorical. All this activity is concerned with the power of speech. Now, as I said before, eirein denotes the use of speech; moreover, Homer often uses the word emêsato, which means 'contrive.' From these two words, then, the lawgiver imposes upon us the name of this god who contrived speech and the use of speech--eirein means 'speak'--and tells us : 'Ye human beings, he who contrived speech (eirein emêsato) ought to be called Eiremes by you.' We, however, have beautified the name, as we imagine, and call him Hermes."
- Plato, Cratylus 400d & 408a ff (trans. Fowler)

Mercury also symbolizes our intelligence. In Aesop's *Fables*, after Zeus creates humans, he has Hermes infuse them with intelligence. Mercury represents not just our IQ or level of intelligence, but the ways in which we use it. Mercury is the planet that will fight its battles with words rather than swords and solve its problems with wits rather than force. Mercury is the planet of the mind and all that goes along with it: our curiosity, our interpretation of sensory input, our ability to perceive patterns and sort information.

Like the metal and the planet, Mercury in astrology is also associated with speed, agility and dexterity. The planet moves swift and agile around the Sun, for to do otherwise would pull him out of his orbit and into the Sun itself. The quicksilver metal moves fast and fluidly, able to take the shape of whatever container it finds itself in. All this reminds us of Hermes, with his winged helmet and sandals, and his penchant for disguise. Mercury in astrology shows our own versatility and ability to adapt to the situations we find ourselves in.

With his swift movement also comes the association with roads and travelers, and Mercury in astrology is concerned with transportation and navigation, especially using the stars as a navigational aid. Which brings to mind one of Hermes' most notable roles as traveler, his role as Psychopomp: guide of souls to the Underworld. In astrology, the orbit of the planet Mercury can be seen as symbolic of Hermes' journeys to the Underworld and back, and of the ability of our minds to take us to different levels of consciousness. Mercury is seen either as a morning or evening star, or not seen at all, invisible due to its closeness to the Sun. It disappears and reappears, as it is never far away from the Sun from our perspective here on Earth.

Mercury's cycle can be divided into two halves: the waxing, morning star half, and the waning, evening star half. Dane Rudhyar, a Humanistic astrologer, called the morning star phase of Mercury the Promethean phase, in honor of the titan Prometheus, known for his foresight and the gift of fire to humanity. He called the evening star phase of Mercury the Epimethean phase, for Prometheus' brother, Epimetheus, known for his hindsight. These phases represent the movement of our minds inward and outward, forward and back: our ability to generate new ideas and concepts, and our ability to reflect upon them and reconsider them.

Also true to myth is Mercury's status as a "trickster" planet. About three times a year, we experience a phenomena called "Mercury Retrograde," for which people blame all sorts of modern calamities such as server crashes, email bounces, car accidents, and all manner of things running off-kilter. A retrograde is when a planet appears to be moving backwards through the sky, from our perspective here on Earth. The planet isn't really moving backwards, and astrologers know this as well as anyone, but it is the symbolic appearance and its meaning that astrology is concerned with. While Mercury Retrograde can coincide with all manner of annoyance and frustration, it generally symbolizes a need to slow down and pay attention, a time for some thoughtful reflection that may lead to us revising our priorities. If we're not using the time wisely, we're more likely to see Hermes' trickster side come out and play.

These are just a few of the many connections between Hermes the god and Mercury the astrological planet. And Mercury itself is just one facet of the symbolic language of astrology. Each of us is born with an astrological chart, filled with planets and other celestial bodies bearing the names and symbols of our beloved gods. I wish you the joy of building your relationship with the gods while exploring the planets who carry their names, symbols and messages. May you find inspiration through the guidance of the stars!

Travels With Hermes:
How to Build a Portable Shrine for the God of Roads
by Rebecca Buchanan

Portable shrines are a great, convenient way for modern Pagans to honor the Gods even while on the go. They are also easy to make: all you need are a few items which remind you of the God or Goddess for whom you are making the shrine, glue, and imagination. Below is my personal recipe for a Hermes portable shrine; alter it as you see fit to create your own, unique shrine in honor of Hermes (or any other Deity of your choice).

Items: one gift card box. Sturdy cardboard boxes, such as those sold by Barnes and Noble, work best; metallic gift card boxes, which can often be found at craft stores, may prove problematic when passing through airport security.

One found coin.

Jewelry charms: bee hive and bee, lock and key, horseshoe, and turtle; each in some way references a myth concerning Hermes or an aspect of his personality.

Black paint, silver paint, brush and bowl of water.

Superglue.

Three stones, flat enough to be stacked.

Building the Shrine:

I opted for a gift card box with a globe and book on the front cover, which are particularly evocative of Hermes. I painted the inside of the box black, calling to mind both Hermes' birth inside a mountain cave, and his connection to the Underworld.

Next, I stacked and glued the three stones on the inside, bottom of the box, creating a miniature, primitive herm. I made sure to hold the stones in place until the glue hardens. (Since the stones are the heaviest items, stacking them on the bottom helps to balance the shrine.)

After arranging and rearranging the jewelry charms and the coin (making sure the box would still close securely), I glued them in place. I connected the hive and bee charms with a short length of chain. Depending on the coin, you may want to glue it reverse side up instead of obverse; in the case of this shrine, I glued the penny in place so that the classically-themed Lincoln Memorial was visible rather than the profile of Lincoln himself.

Finally, I took the silver paint and drew a petasus (winged helmet) against the black background.

That's it! The portable shrine is small enough to tuck inside my carry-on bag, where I can keep both an eye on it and keep I handy; I would hate to lose it if an airport inspector considered it contraband or my luggage was misplaced. When I am at home, the portable shrine sits on my main altar, beside my icons of Hermes.

Hopefully, my own recipe has given you a few ideas for creating a portable shrine of your own. Now get to it!

Maia
by P. Sufenas Virius Lupus

Daughter of Atlas, nymph most kind
that in Kyllenian cave bore
a child of greatest fortune's find —
today it is she I adore!

O flowering Fauna, ever fair,
fragrantly luring Kronos' son
to sport with sweetest tresséd hair
before the sleep of Hera's done.

In that hard cave's obscurity
you gave him, unassisted, birth;
from godly lack and poverty
the cattle-stealer made much mirth.

With fire-wielding Vulcan's might
you are now mingled properly;
with Mercury's geminate sight
your month is ruled celestially.

Therefore, upon us mortals weak
give grandeur despite circumstance,
and succor to all those who seek
to not be at mercy of chance.

It is with dances and with song
and fruit and blossom you return —
may we who live not forget long
your name as summer's fires burn.

Great Maia, mother of Hermes,
upon these verses do not look
with scorn, nor curses, should they please,
and bless the pages of this book!

A Musician's Prayer to Hermes
by Rebecca Buchanan

Hermes
Playful God
Who found music
      hidden in the shell of a tortoise:
bless my song

Hymn to Hermes I
by Sarenth Odinsson

They destroyed your works and destroyed your words
Yet, ever on they flow
The crash of walls and burnt parchment
Still, it fills the nose
The weeps of those who knew your name
The echoes of their woe
Still fills the ears, the heart, the soul
Yet your glory do we know
The script and speech, we know them well
Your seeds that you have sewn
The messages that build belief
The Gods whose mouths you've shown
The hope and love, the dross and hate
The words have only grown
That gift you daily gift to us
The building of small stones
The palace that you build in us
The place that we call home
Blessed one, O Messenger
Hear my call and know
That we still speak your words and deeds
In us you have your own

Hymn to Hermes II
by Sarenth Odinsson

Your name is known to many and your words are
spoken yet
Come, let your words fill us
Your deeds are still taught from school and home alike
Come, let your skills teach us
Your words are taught in hope and dream
Come, let your will mold us

Your eyes see every hidden place
Come, let your vision see us
Your feet walk every occult road
Come, let your stride guide us
Your hands are full of cunning
Come, let your hands free us
Your lips of full of wisdom
Come, let your lips instruct us
Your ears are laden with the words of all
Come, let your ears hear us

Hymn to Hermes III
by Sarenth Odinsson

Great glorious one who dared to walk in places far and
    wide
The path you tread is the place where your holiness
    abides
The roads that wind about the lands like snakes and
    serpents old
Those places where the mysteries of your people will
    unfold
The depth of earth and height of sky and all places in
    between
The stretches where you walk in power, the seen and yet
    unseen
The humbled heart and the proud fool, all you speak
    unto
The ignorant would gain the world if only they would
    hear you
The downtrodden and the happiest, all can hear your
    voice
The clarion call could pierce them all if they would make
    the choice
The holy one who walks to and from wherever He may
    please
The one who we hold in pietas, Hail Holy Hermes!

44 Adorations of Hermes
by Rebecca Buchanan

I sing
I sing
I sing
he who is
Bearer of the Golden Wand
Born on Mount Cyllene
Bringer of Luck
Cattle-Slayer
Companion of Heroes
Comrade of the Feast
Cunning Guide
Devious Rogue
Enveloped in Craft and Deceit
Friend of Dionysus
Full of Wiles
Giver of Good Things
Glad-Hearted
Glorious
Guardian of the Marketplace
Guide of Dreams
Honey-Tongued
Inventor of the Lyre
Keeper of Boars With Gleaming Tusks
Knot-Maker
Lord of All Birds of Good Omen
Master of Fierce-Eyed Lions
Messenger of the Gods
Mischievous One
Prince of Thieves
Protector of Strangers
Psychopomp

Quicksilver
Ram-Bearer
Rich in Flocks
Robber
Sharp-Eyed
Shepherd
Slayer of Argus
Sly-Hearted Cheat
Son of Maia
Spy in the Night
The Strong Son of Zeus
Three-Headed
Tortoise-Killer
Trickster
Watcher at the Door
Winning in His Cleverness
he who is
I sing
I sing
I sing

The Account of Hermaphroditos
by P. Sufenas Virius Lupus

We are them that is called androgyne.

We were the son of Hermes of swift feet
and Aphrodite of the curling hair.

Idaean nymphs were our fosterers.

Yet, a nymph was also ourself
of the flowing springs of Caria.

Forth from the cave at fifteen we came.

Salmakis we were called when combing
our hair in pool reflection, a female Narcissus.

We looked up from the mirror and saw ourself.

We were beautiful, and falling in love was instant,
but we were only thirsty and wanting water.

We had hair as beautiful as our mother's.

We were a spritely smooth-skinned youth,
with full flesh that fascinated.

We convinced ourself that a bath was desirable.

We were already naked wandering the woods,
for in watery life we never owned clothes.

Water washed us, cleansed our separation.

Now look upon us, for we are union,
eternally one, never dual.

Fast as Hermes, fierce as Aphrodite.

Look on us with love's longing,
and watch us slip away quickly.

We are the interpreter of love.

With Hermes' member we engender,
we are mother to all with these breasts.

We are the brother and sister to Priapus and Erotes.

We have been in every body on earth,
yet many have hidden us ashamed away.

We build our altar of flesh and fluids.

We are not pleased with the sacrifices
men have given and have failed to give.

All those in love wish to become us.

But better to realize in being yourselves
you in your unity already are us.

Trickster
by Samantha Chapman

I've always been drawn to Tricksters. I have known the stories since I was a little girl, known their names: Mercury, Anansi, Loki, Coyote. I have read everything about them that I could get my hands on. Other gods in their pantheons occasionally found my interest, but the Tricksters were always my favorites. A long time ago, I tried to worship them, the way small children do. I was a mischievous child to begin with, and I justified my actions to my elders by calling it religion. It never worked, but I kept trying. I dedicated my graffiti to Loki, my practical jokes to Coyote, and as I played I prayed to them, one at a time, all at once, each in turn. Eventually I outgrew the more blatant pranks, and my interest in the gods became more academic, but never faded entirely. In the back of my mind they were always there, encouraging me, fascinating me, driving me on. And then one day, I learned why.

I didn't have to try to find him. He wasn't any of the gods I'd read about, from far-off places and distant times. For years the city had brimmed with the energy of the people who lived there, and it had borne its own gods into the world. That was always a comforting idea, as my schooling dragged on. Just a Bachelor's, I'd told myself, then why not a Masters? I was halfway through my PhD by now. A scholar of ancient literature and mythology, ready to unleash my books on an unsuspecting public. But it wasn't meant to be, not then. I had something much more important to learn.

He looked like he belonged, no matter where he stood. I never would have pegged him for a deity, but it was the eyes that convinced me. The clothes were simple:

a tattered, well-loved jacket hugged his shoulders. His jeans were faded artfully, broken to soft, supple perfection. He wore his hair just long enough for a ponytail, and wore his face fresh and smooth. He could have been in my college classroom, or reading poetry at the coffee shop down the block, or driving the subway trains deep under the sidewalk, and he would have looked just as in place. But his eyes ...when he let me look into them closely, I could see it. The way the universe spun inside them, where most people only had the wheels of their own minds. The way they flickered with black fire, giving him the light to see the world the way it really was.

When he needed to, he called himself Dmitri. But even the first time I heard it, I knew that it wasn't his true name, or his only one. He introduced himself as if we should have been old friends, stopping me on the sidewalk without hesitating or causing any fuss. "Hello, Vivian." I felt a chill run up my spine when he said my name. "It's time we had a little talk."

He started to walk without looking back, and I followed him, not yet knowing why he had such a pull. The more I thought the more I remembered seeing him, on the street, in the bookstore where I worked, in the clusters of students around campus. He had wormed his way into my life, and I never noticed. But I trusted him already, enough to go with him to a small, secluded glade that I'd never seen in the park before.

I tried to just look nonchalant, like there wasn't something about him that made me burn with curiosity, but I couldn't stop looking over every inch of him and he had to have noticed.

He chuckled. Through our whole talk he kept chuckling, like it was just a part of his rich tenor voice.

134

Like he was just constantly amused at the way the world worked. "Do you know who I am?"

"I think I've got a hunch," I murmured, still trying to identify the feeling that I had in his presence, of awe and smallness and potential. "You're not human."

"No. But am I so very far from it?"

I reached out to touch him, and that was when I looked into his eyes. My fingers landed on his smooth cheek, sliding down his neck to the faded jacket and feeling the warm body beneath. "No ..." I could almost piece it together, if my mind would just accept what I was learning.

"You've been quite devout ... well, as much as my kind expect," he said, and I thought back to all the studies of my childhood, all the studies I'd kept doing, all the papers I'd written on archetypes and pantheons. "You know what I am. Or if you don't, you've been a very poor student, and not worth my precious time."

"God ... you really are, aren't you?" I asked in a whisper, silently chastising myself for the oath. "You are a god ... you're one of them, one of the — "

"Tricksters," he grinned. He started to pace, taking slow, even steps all around me. "And you ... do you know what you are?"

I felt his eyes on the back of my neck, going straight through my sweater, straight through my skin. "Well I'm human, for one."

He stopped when he reached my face again, giving me that amused smile. "Yes, you are. Like so many others. A human girl, with a good simple life that's never been enough. I've heard your prayers, Vivian," he told me, smile never slipping. "You prayed by getting to know us. You prayed by seeking knowledge, looking for larger truth. Simple facts, they're just never enough for the likes of us."

"Us?"

"I've seen people like you a thousand times, in a thousand lifetimes," he continued, barely even hearing my question. "Wearing a thousand faces, but the dreams are always the same. You want ... you simply want. Something more. Something different."

"Where are you going with this?" I felt my pulse fluttering. Somehow, I already thought I knew.

"I'm going to offer you a gamble, Vivian. With that solid, steady, dull life of yours on the line." He started to pace again, his gait more fluid with every step. "All these years you've learned and waited and wanted. So here's your chance. Your trial. I'm offering you all you ever dreamed."

"Why?" I asked him. I couldn't be too excited, not yet. I had to push down the bubbling giddiness in my stomach. If he truly was what he said, I couldn't let myself be tricked. "You really want to do that for me? To, what, to test me? And what do I get if I pass?"

"You come out on the other side more than you are now," he answered. "I can show you things you never imagined you could do. And if you win, they're yours, for the rest of your life. But if you fail your tests," he continued, wagging a finger in front of my face, "then you must give up your old life to me. There's so very much I could do with an ordinary girl," he said with such a sly delight. "You could gain everything, or lose all you ever had. Or you could walk away," he added with a shrug. "And live out that dull life like nothing ever happened."

I swallowed to clear the lump out of my throat as I tried to think. He was watching me, his two eyes so heavy on my skin, the gaze of all the world in one man.

"Why me?" I asked him softly, and as the question sprouted in my mind it bloomed its own answer. "Why offer this to me, if there are so many others? If I'm that dull, that common? Why me, if I'm that ordinary?"

He only smiled, nodding once, and I knew that I knew the answer.

"I'll do it."

*****

All was dark, here. It could have been a week after our meeting, or an hour, or a year. Time moved differently. The air all around me crackled with the energy of a new universe, electricity that didn't need electrons, thoughts floating through the ether with no thinker. My breaths were slow, but every second saw a full tornado's worth of wind cycle through my lungs.

The rules were different, here.

When my eyes opened I stared into the dark, not moving, but the emptiness was too much to bear standing in one place. I started to walk, although I couldn't tell what direction I was going. The same dreary curtain of blackness hung everywhere I looked. If I squinted, I could see the horizon line where the darkness should have ended, but no matter how far I walked I couldn't get any closer. When I turned my head to look back, the opposite side wasn't any farther away. I stopped again, and took a deeper breath. Wandering blindly wouldn't get me anywhere. Instead, I called out to the one who had to be watching. "What do you want out of me?"

The silence answered me. I could still feel his heavy eyes, and I listened for directions that weren't coming. The silence came from all directions, pressing in on me, keeping me in the same small place. It dawned on me that I already was where I needed to be. I just couldn't see what I needed to do. I sank down to the floor – at least there *was* a floor – and crossed my legs underneath me.

The ground below me was the only solid thing I could find. But this place, this world, couldn't be empty. That would be far too boring for a Trickster. There wouldn't be any point to trapping me in nothingness, with no way to get out. His fun came from watching me try, from wondering whether I would figure it out. If there were really nothing I could do, there would be nothing for him to amuse himself by watching. And nothing for me to learn from it all.

"You wanted to give me a challenge," I murmured, knowing he was listening. "This is a pretty lame one."

I thought I could feel his laughter in the air, but he didn't answer me in words. I tapped my foot against the floor, focusing just on my breathing, waiting for the inspiration to strike me. The ground was smooth as marble, warm as thick carpet, soft as silk, all at once. I stopped tapping, when something finally came to mind. I reached out to draw my fingers across the floor, feeling it out more carefully. When I thought of cushioning, it yielded to my touch; it stood firm when I wanted support. I let my thoughts go wilder, testing, seeing how far I could take this. In turns, the ground beneath me turned to grass, to bean-bag, to rippling water.

"That's it …." I laughed out loud, giddy with my discovery. Reaching out again, I willed the darkness all around me to form the way that I needed, the way that I wanted, shaping the world. "I need to see …."

My hand closed on the handle of an old oil

lantern, and everything changed.

By the lamplight I could hear his applause. I could feel his pride hanging in the air, draping around me like a blanket. The world bloomed into life all around me, so much more revealed by my little lantern than I should have been able to see. But the light of my oil brought the sunrise, and we stood together in a wide-open field, soft velvet grass embroidered with daisies. I looked up and saw the stars, the planets, all the universe playfully winking at me past the frost of a daytime sky.

"Very good ... very, very good." His voice purred in my ear, tingling over the back of my neck. He stood behind me, barely an inch away, and his fingers closed over my arms, holding me still. "I knew you'd get this far. Still, it delights me that you can see what I've built for you."

"Was that my challenge?" I didn't look back at him. My gaze was fixed out at the beautiful land before me, but I could still see his face just past the corner of my eye.

"One challenge," he answered. The excitement, the energy that a less-dignified man would have spent bouncing up and down simply flowed from his fingers into my skin. "You've gotten this far but it's hardly over, my dear. How do you like this world of yours?" he asked, stretching his arm out to show me the whole thing. "You've learned how to use it, how to build it. A gift, from me." I finally turned around and saw his smile, pearl-white and gleaming with something between pride and mischief. "And now, you are in my debt."

"What, you mean I have to stay here? You're kidnapping me?" I thought back to all the fairy stories I used to read, and it didn't seem unlikely.

Once again, he laughed at my question. "Call it

what you will. Of course, to get out of that debt, all you need to do is give me something in return. Give me something that I value, as much as you value all of this." He let go then, and stepped away from me, leaving me to figure the rest out on my own.

I tried to breathe deeply, to collect my thoughts all over again. The air was so sweet, so clear. The whole place was magnificent, but its beauty wasn't why I valued it, to use his word. I loved it for what it meant to me. This world meant that all the dreams I used to dream were true. It meant that there was magic in the world, and I could find it. It meant that there was something about me interesting enough to catch a god's attention. With the clapping of his hands in the darkness, he had given my whole life a new meaning, given me the adventure my younger self was so sure I would have. My spirits soared when I first saw his gift, but they started to sink now. What could I possibly give him that he would love this much?

Those heavy eyes lingered on the back of my neck for a very long time, while I stepped out into the paradise. I made sure not to look back at him. I wasn't about to ask for his help, or his mercy, or whatever someone weaker might do. There was a way for me to win this, and I just had to find it. I came to rest at the foot of a glittering brook that ran through my field. I stared into the water and moved my hands the way that I had in the darkness, idly molding the water into shapes and making them dance in the air.

What could a god want? He had power, so much power. He could make anything that he wanted for himself, the same way he made this for me. He wasn't bound by the constraints that normal people had, by work and school and family. He had no obligations to escape from. He was free already to do anything he pleased, for any reason, whenever he wished.

My fingers curled in the grass underneath me, and suddenly I knew what to do.

First I needed to change ... I had still been wearing the rumpled jeans and sweater that he found me in, and they wouldn't be any help for the idea forming in my mind. I stretched my legs out in front of me and held the fabric of my jeans together, until the two legs melded into one skirt, and the fabric grew soft and shimmered. The same for my top: the plain cotton turned to silk at my touch, and I dotted my chest with jewels. When I stood, my new gown hugged my body, soft lilac trailing off into wisps of nothingness by the time it hit my knees. I finally looked back at him, and saw the look of eager curiosity in those eyes.

"That's certainly an interesting guess." He looked me up and down, and started to come closer. "But women are nothing new to me. Are you sure this is what you want to offer?"

My hand closed behind my back, and felt the length of rope that I had conjured, rough and heavy in my palm. He should have been able to sense it, in this world of his. But his distracted gaze raked over me from head to toe. "I could still surprise you."

"If anyone could," he agreed, stepping up nearer. He trailed his hand on my shoulder, feeling out the lines of my neck. "An arrogant girl. I like that. But I might well be convinced to call us even."

He leaned forward and I moved carefully, letting my own free hand fall on his arm, and stepping around him. Slowly, I circled him fully, never taking my touch away. "Why not let me show you what I can do to you?" I whispered, halting my steps when I stood at his back.

"Oh yes," he breathed, his eyes closing, his guard down. Without rushing, I reached for one of his hands, then the other, bringing them both together at the small of his back. I could feel him burning, with curiosity, with desire.

Before he had the chance to open his eyes again, I had him. I slid the rope around his wrists and fastened it tightly, all in one fluid movement. His eyes flashed with fury as he spun to look at me again, but it was too late. I let him go, and I could see how hard he was struggling against the rope. He couldn't get free. With the power he had given to me, I reached my hand to shape the earth, pulling thick bars up around him into a fast iron cage.

"What have you done?" He threw himself at the bars, as best as he could with his hands behind his back. I saw him try to cover up a stumble, and his eyes blazed brighter than they ever had before, full of anger ... more importantly, full of fear.

"I didn't have anything you wanted." My breath was faster, and his easy chuckle slipped into my voice. "You have everything ... and if you don't have it, you can make it, and if you can't make it, you can steal it. Except you can't, now. Because I've trapped you ... because you gave me control over my own power, didn't you?" I grinned wider, watching him stop his struggle. "You can't do anything against the things I make ... you could break them with your own, maybe, but not without your hands. You gave me the same power you have, the same strength." I stepped closer to his bars. The fact that his hands were still trapped by my rope confirmed everything I had said. I looked into his eyes one more time, and this time their power didn't intimidate me. "So I have what you want. What you value. Your power, and the freedom to use it. It's mine, to give back to you."

For a long, tense moment he stared back at me, searching for some way that I could be wrong. When he fully realized what I had done, he shook his head, looking downward and smiling. "I knew I chose right. You are a remarkable girl."

"Then I've won?"

"You've won," he admitted, his head tilted forward in defeat. "Now let me free?"

The feeling of matter changing a yard away as I worked my hands in the air was something I would never forget, even if I wanted to. I urged the iron bars to turn back to soil and pressed them back into the earth. With a flick of my wrist the rope around his hands turned into a tiny brown sparrow and flew off into the world, to enjoy its own freedom.

"And a masterful finishing touch," he complimented me, watching the little bird soar away. "You have learned well, haven't you? All I had to do was give you the tools to show yourself off."

"I learned from the best," I told him, and this time when he walked up close to me, I looked him straight on. "And I've been learning for a long time."

The gown that I had made was still draped around me, and he started to play with it, gently teasing the silk between his fingers. "You've impressed me."

"I knew I could." Words that might have sounded arrogant from my lips just a few days ago suddenly felt right at home.

"And you deserve to be rewarded," he continued without missing a beat. "Something unique ... something worth you ... how about this?" He stretched his arms out and gestured all around him.

It took me a moment to understand his offer. "All

143

this?" I asked, glancing in every direction at the paradise that spread into infinity.

"It's yours, if you choose to accept it." This time I watched that smile more closely. There was something different ... not about him, but about me. I could see more carefully, think more clearly. When I didn't answer right away, he added, "It won't put you in my debt, not this time. To have you accept, to have you stay here, is payment enough for me."

My eyes narrowed as I considered his offer. I could stay here, and it would be beautiful. I could live my whole life out in this world he built for me, molding corners of it to suit my demands, never wanting for anything. It could be perfect, a life I always dreamed of having. But another thought made me pause. The world would be perfect, but it would be a cage. It would be his magic, not mine. And just as he had been trapped in my bars, I'd be in prison, here. His songbird, his pet, his prize.

Before now, I had never been excited to return home. But I looked down at my hands, and my mind whizzed with possibility. Anything I ever wanted to do was in my power. I could see what the world looked like from the top of a mountain, or the bottom of the sea. If I didn't want to, I'd never have to work again; people like him ... people like us never seemed to need money. I could go anywhere I wanted and with the flick of my wrist, have anything I needed. I could learn to work people, learn what makes them tick, and how to make them tock the way I wished. Before now, home was a place of simplicity and predictability. My world would never be predictable again.

"I'd rather live my own life."

My words made the sunlight flicker, and his

144

world started to fade away. In one way his smile fell, but in another it brightened, both at once. The scenery fell away into a thousand million shooting stars around us, taking us back to the unformed darkness. As his sky melted, I felt a weight come off of my shoulders that I had never noticed was there.

"Very well, Vivian. I must admit, you've made me proud." He reached out his fingers one last time, and now I let him move them to my hair. They tangled through it, the tender touch of a final meeting. "I'll put you back where I found you. You've passed all my tests. You've earned your reward." I hadn't expected the sadness in his voice, but I could feel the way he thought. Without me for a plaything, he would find another, and soon forget his loss. His fingers moved to my eyes and closed the lids, and I felt everything around me start to spin. When he let go, the weight of his eyes remained on mine for a long while.

*****

It had started to rain, somewhere in the time that we had been together. When I was returned to my side of the world, I just stood still and let it fall on me. I had never felt the rain like this before. Every drop held the memory of every part of the earth it had ever traveled over as a cloud. When I finally got tired of feeling the rain, I flicked my wrist. An umbrella clicked into life in my hand and I swung it over my head, smiling as I walked into the world.

Antinous Neos Hermes
by P. Sufenas Virius Lupus

Some will sing of Antinous
as "Epiphanios" or "Choreios,"
he who appears, he who dances;

some will call him "Pythios,"
the oracular inspirer,
a Belenus for youth and beauty;

some will chant "Antinosiris"
and "Osirantinous" daily,
the Nile's mysterious one;

but I sing not of he who moves,
or he who comes or speaks,
nor he who conquers death.

I sing of the new Argus–slayer,
the one who with deftness
destroys the all–seeing terror.

I sing of the Arcadian
who hunts and herds and steals
in and to and from the underworld.

I sing of the hero at the gate
who is not initiated
because he has already seen.

I sing of the New Hermes,
the son of the great god,
the emissary.

But no mere messenger,
the one who is exchange
and reciprocity as well.

He who stands between
seer and what is seen,
sound and listener.

He who gives and takes,
buys and sells, carries,
bridges boundaries.

He is there where visions are,
he is there where words sound,
he is there where hearts stir.

But more, he is between
image and eye, ear and music,
lover and beloved and love.

He is a god most alive
when he is used, employed
to engage the world.

To interpret, to intercede,
he is hermeneusis
and epistemics.

He is a son of Hermes,
rejuvenated by Thoth,
favored by Re–Harakhte.

It is no hymn I make,
no song to sweetly sing,
no rhymes to write,

for how can one convey
that who one is conveying
is how one conveys it ...

Hermes Haiku I
by Rebecca Buchanan

he is the four-faced
watcher in
the night, silver-eyed

Hermes in America
by Jennifer Lawrence

I.

No borders out of ancient myth and tale
Could keep him bound up within just one land;
Swift-footed one made up his mind one day
To travel far from home and see the world.
Caduceus in hand, he hit the road —
"I've worshippers I think I'll go to see;
I'm sure they'd like a visit there from me."
The ocean was no bar to his deft feet:
Talaria to whisk him over waves;
When he touched down, his soles were dry as bone
Baked hot in desert kiln for many years.
He cast his eyes about, grinning ear to
Ear: "Where shall I start? Who should I visit
First?" A penny glinted at his feet; he
Bent, picked it up, tossed it high in air, and
Caught it, slapped down on arm — "North it is, then,
To Boston shall I wend, and go to see
Those who love me there." And so he traveled
On, doing little tricks along the way:
A dying soul eased to the afterlife,
Stumbling speaker given tongue of silver;
Money unforeseen for a starving man.
Spreading luck and aid along the way, he
Came at last to Boston's antique byways.

II.

He walks here, has a hot dog, takes in some
History, plays with children. So much to
See, and he could spend forever seeing
It. But he has a purpose, and one by
One, he visits followers, whispering
Quietly into their ears, brushing them
With luck, smiling unseen, happy just to
Be. One woman finds a new job, out of
The blue, idiot-free, doing what she
Loves. A man skilled in Ares' ways stops near an
Alley just in time to stop a crime most
Foul. All around the city Hermes goes,
And in several of the nearby towns,
Too, sowing fortune and circumstance in
His path, before He thinks of moving on.

III.

Not far from Boston he stopped a little
While in Baltimore, murmuring words of
Encouragement and love into the ear
Of one who'd followed Him for many years.
Dark was the fog that dragged at that one's soul,
And gentle was His hand as He tarried,
Patient but firm, understanding of his
Troubles and fears, as are all lovers with
Their beloved. And when His spouse had come
To that place of calm decision, only
Then did Hermes at last turn and move on.

IV.

Wherever people worshipped Him, he stopped,
Even if just for a while, to listen
To what they had to say, to hold their hands,
To hear their sorrows and their joys. He knew
He could not stay on Earth forever; Mount
Olympus needed Him, Zeus needed Him,
But for a time, the messages would wait.
He spent a day in Memphis, another
In Alabama, spoke with a poet
In Arkansas. In Michigan, He spent
The night watching movies with an old friend,
And moved on to a girl like honey in
Colorado. Minnesota kept Him
Busy; He danced from city to city,
Savoring the time He was with each of
His children. And always He moved onward.

V.

The Midwest is wide, but His sandals were
Big enough to cross it without trouble.
Chicago took Him longest; so many
People there, calling His name, and sometimes
Not even knowing it. In one home, He
Watched a ritual to His brother, the
One whose bounteous flocks He had stolen;
The longing in the hearts of those who prayed
Was sweet as wine, and the scent of laurel
On the wind. He left them with a blessing
And a laugh, and headed on, to visit
Another, weaving through the walls of books
To brush a gentle kiss against her brow.

VI.

At last He came to stop where the salt spray
Of the Western ocean cascades into
The air, cleansing all it touches, driving
Miasma away. The sweet green scent of
Forest lingered in the air: He could feel
His sister the Huntress near, and smiled as
He headed to visit a couple who
Had held Him in their hearts for a long time.
Their prayers wreathed round His ears; their gifts
    brought
A smile to His eyes. He walked with them for
A day, into the woods and the hills, and
Though He never let them catch a glimpse of
Him, He knew that they understood that He
Walked at their side. Wine and bread and honey
They gave for Him. He ate, and was content.

VII.

But, in the end, He knew the time was near when
He had to return; knew Olympus would
Not wait forever. He did not wish to
Leave; friend to mankind, closest to us in
So many ways, happiest perhaps when
He moves among us unseen, but still, He
Knew he had to go. Reluctantly, then,
He bid farewell to the hills and roads He
Had traveled, said goodbye to the land that
Lay between Poseidon's waves, and once more
Launched himself up, into the brilliant blue,
To answer duty, and His father's call.

But of course, He can never stay away.

Hermes Prayer
by K.S. Roy

Luck and loss
Two sides of the same coin
Which face will you show to me?
Dreamers tend to gamble
And risk more than we can afford
Just for a shot at winning the prize ...

Luck will find me
When I least expect it
When your star rises in the morning
And smiles upon my upturned face
Hopeful and waiting anxiously
For the favor of your guidance

Lead me on, Ram Bearer
I'll strain to hear you whispers
On this tangled highway
Looking to the stars to find my way
And feeling that subtle aura of your presence
Knowing you walk beside me.

Our Contributors

Audrey Anastasi cannot remember a time when she did not have a paintbrush or pencil in her hand.

A curator, gallery owner/director, educator and arts advocate, Audrey Frank Anastasi is, above all else, a tireless and dedicated working artist. She has an extensive history of exhibiting her artwork in the United States and abroad. Ms. Anastasi received her BFA from the University of Miami on full academic scholarship, majoring in painting, and minoring in photography. She moved to Brooklyn to attend Pratt Institute, where she received her MFA majoring in painting, and minoring in art history.

Working is a variety of media, Ms. Anastasi works quickly and intuitively, to allow surprise in her process and in the viewer. One of the unusual aspects of her process, is that although Audrey is right-handed, she has switched to working with her left hand, almost exclusively, for all the figure and portrait work. Accepting the challenge of using the non-dominant left hand enabled her to reconnect with the physicality of the paint stroke, and to redirect attention to the soul of the subject matter.

For more, visit www.AudreyAnastasi.com.

Christa A. Bergerson has been worshipping and adoring the wondrous Roman-Greco-Egyptian Gods since she was a precocious tot. She is an occultist, an environmentalist, and a Guardian of those who writhe betwixt the veil. In her spare time, she also enjoys listening to phonographs, traversing the sparse wilds of Illinois, and swimming in the dead of night. Her poetry has appeared or will appear in *Waters of Life, Bearing Torches, The Beltane Papers, The Gunpowder Review, Abyss and Apex Magazine of Speculative Fiction, Kaleidotrope,* and *Faerie Nation Magazine,* among other publications. For astral and/or sublunary communication feel free to contact her at carmentaeternus@comcast.net.

Amanda Sioux Blake is the keeper of the Temple of Athena the Savior, Alexandrian Tradition, and the author of *Ink In My Veins: A Collection of Contemporary Pagan Poetry* and *Songs of Praise: Hymns to the Gods of Greece.* She is currently working on the forthcoming *Journey to Olympos: A Modern Spiritual Odyssey.*

A self-labeled history geek, she has taught classes on Greek Mythology and has written the coursework for "Olympos in Egypt", an introduction to the unique hybrid culture and spiritually that grew up in Alexandria, Egypt in the Hellenistic Age. If you are interested, email her at starsong_dragon@yahoo.com. She also runs an online T-shirt store specializing in Greek and Egyptian designs, as well as general Pagan and fantasy, which can be found here: http://www.cafepress.com/other_world.

Amanda currently splits her time between school in Tucson, AZ and her home in South Bend, Indiana with her boyfriend of six years and the various animals that are her companions. She has been 'officially' Pagan for over a decade, since age twelve or thirteen, but remembers being called by Athena at age seven. She spends most of her time reading, writing, teaching, painting, worshiping the Gods, working on her many projects, and caring for the far too many animals that find their way to her home.

Rebecca Buchanan is the Editor-in-Chief of *Bibliotheca Alexandrina*. She is also the editor of the literary ezine, *Eternal Haunted Summer*, and she blogs regularly at *BookMusings: (Re)Discovering Pagan Literature*. She has been previously published in such venues as *Cliterature*, *Luna Station Quarterly*, *Bards and Sages Quarterly*, *Datura: An Anthology of Esoteric Poesis* (*Scarlet Imprint*), *Hex Magazine*, and other venues.

Samantha Chapman is a recent graduate from the Medieval and Renaissance Studies program at NYU. She has nursed a lifelong interest in mythology and fantasy, and is thrilled to see her work in print for the first time. She would love to hear feedback, and can be reached at smc510@nyu.edu.

Ariana Dawnhawk has been pursuing magic and the edges of things for a long time, sometimes without realizing it. She is an eclectic striving for syncretism and a professional creative, who seems to attract nouned adjectives. Her influences include Feri, Morningstar, Eclectic/NeoWicca, Thelema, and a small group focused on teaching and learning called the Department, which was the beginning of her magical path. Her spiritual passions include devotional work in everyday life and connection with the community of Beings. She is active in her local OTO body.

Solongo Dulaan is a High Priestess in the Hellenic Alexandrian tradition and a shamaness in the Mongolian tradition of Tengerism. Her blog can be found at theeagleflight.com. She is a follower of the Orphic

157

Mysteries. It is her joy to write, sing, dance, and pray in honour of the gods. In love and light she wishes to share this joy and happiness with others. Chara kai Eudaimonia!

Jason Ross Inczauskis recently completed his Masters degree and is residing close to Chicago, Illinois. He currently lives in a small apartment with his love, Tabitha, his pet plant, Audrey the Immortal, and more books and dolls than you can shake a stick at. He is a fairly recent convert to Hellenismos despite a long-held fascination with the Greek Gods. When asked about his spiritual path, he may refer to himself as a Hellene, a Hellenic, or Greek Pre-Orthodox, depending on who's asking and his mood at the time, though he always follows it with the caveat: 'but not a very good one'. He has worshipped Athena for many years, but now honors the other Hellenic deities as well.

Galina Krasskova is a Heathen priest and Northern Tradition shaman who is currently pursuing a PhD in classics. She is the author of over a dozen books and may be found lurking and causing trouble at http://krasskova.weebly.com.

Jennifer Lawrence has been following Hermes a very long time. Some of the places He has led her her have been good ones, some have been sad, but none of them have been boring. She looks forward to following Him all the rest of the way, down to that last journey together.

P. Sufenas Virius Lupus is one of the founding members of the Ekklesía Antínoou – a queer, Graeco-Roman-Egyptian syncretist reconstructionist polytheist group dedicated to Antinous, the deified lover of the Roman Emperor Hadrian, and related deities and divine figures – as well as a contributing member of Neos Alexandria and a practicing Celtic Reconstructionist pagan in the traditions of gentlidecht and filidecht, as well as Romano-British, Welsh, and Gaulish deity devotions. Lupus is also dedicated to several land spirits around the area of North Puget Sound and its islands. Lupus' work (poetry, fiction, and essays) has appeared in a number of *Bibliotheca Alexandrina* devotional volumes, as well as Ruby Sara's anthologies *Datura* (2010) and *Mandragora* (2012), Inanna Gabriel and C. Bryan Brown's *Etched Offerings* (2011), Lee Harrington's *Spirit of Desire: Personal Explorations of Sacred Kink* (2010), and Galina Krasskova's *When the Lion Roars* (2011). Lupus has also written several full-length books, including *The Phillupic Hymns* (2008), *The Syncretisms of Antinous* (2010), *Devotio Antinoo: The Doctor's Notes, Volume One* (2011), *All-Soul, All-Body, All-Love, All-Power: A TransMythology* (2012), and *A Garland for Polydeukion* (2012), with more on the way.

Sarenth Odinsson, aka Timothy Schneider, is a Northern Tradition shaman, and priest of Odin and Anubis. He serves the Pagan community, and anyone who needs his services, as a shaman, priest, writer, spiritual counselor, and diviner. He sees his primary job is to connect people to their Gods and spirits, Ancestors and the Dead and does not discriminate based on gender, sexuality, religion, or path. He has recently reached out to Hermes, and is developing a deeper relationship with Him.

Hélio Pires is a Roman polytheist, historian, blogger, and dog-friend from Portugal. Give him a rock, one that doesn't fit in his pocket, and he'll likely pile it with others on the road-side.

Michael Routery is a writer and poet living in San Francisco. He operates in the liminal zones of Celtic and Hellenic polytheisms. His work can be found in a wide variety of publications, including *Beatitude 50, Datura, Mandragora,* and the *Bibliotheca Alexandrina* devotional anthologies *Written In Wine, Bearing Torches, Unbound, Out of Arcadia,* and *The Scribing Ibis.* He can also be found at finnchuillsmast@wordpress.

K.S. Roy (also known as Khryseis Astra) is an artist, astrologer and writer living in Western Pennsylvania. She is particularly devoted to Hekate, Hermes, Persephone, Apollon and the Muses but also honors the rest of the Theoi as a practitioner of Hellenismos. She is the Graphic Designer for *He Epistole,* a Hellenic Polytheist newsletter issued by Neokoroi, and is currently at work on a new devotional art series for the Theoi.

Melia Suez is a wife, a mother and dedicated to Zeus. She discovered writing when she discovered this spiritual path. Her works are a tribute to not only the chosen subject but also to Hermes. She edited the devotional volume *From Cave to Sky: A Devotional Anthology in Honor of Zeus,* also from BA. Her personal blog is 4ofwands.wordpress.com.

D. L. Wood was a writer, fine artist, and spirit worker. She had been devoted to Hermes Angelos specifically since 2010, and considered Him a Patron. Other Deities she was devoted to include Pythian Apollon and Pallas Athene. She worked on the land in Missouri at a commune helping the various spirits and also spent her time reading and studying esoteric traditions. She had been a Hellenic Polytheist for two years but considered herself only having found what had been inside of her all her life. She kept a website for Hellenic Practice and blog at www.argeiphontes.com. She also offered spiritual counseling and tarot, as well as runes readings and past life readings as well as Oracular work for Pythian Apollon. Tragically, she passed away before this work was released.

About Bibliotheca Alexandrina

Ptolemy Soter, the first Makedonian ruler of Egypt, established the library at Alexandria to collect all of the world's learning in a single place. His scholars compiled definitive editions of the Classics, translated important foreign texts into Greek, and made monumental strides in science, mathematics, philosophy and literature. By some accounts over a million scrolls were housed in the famed library, and though it has long since perished due to the ravages of war, fire, and human ignorance, the image of this great institution has remained as a powerful inspiration down through the centuries.

To help promote the revival of traditional polytheistic religions we have launched a series of books dedicated to the ancient gods of Greece and Egypt. The library is a collaborative effort drawing on the combined resources of the different elements within the modern Hellenic and Kemetic communities, in the hope that we can come together to praise our gods and share our diverse understandings, experiences and approaches to the divine.

A list of our current and forthcoming titles can be found on the following page. For more information on the Bibliotheca, our submission requirements for upcoming devotionals, or to learn about our organization, please visit us at neosalexandria.org.

Sincerely,
The Editorial Board
of the Library of Neos Alexandria

162

Current Titles

Written in Wine:
 A Devotional Anthology for Dionysos
Dancing God:
 Poetry of Myths and Magicks
Goat Foot God
Longing for Wisdom:
 The Message of the Maxims
The Phillupic Hymns
Unbound:
 A Devotional Anthology for Artemis
Waters of Life:
 A Devotional Anthology for Isis and Serapis
Bearing Torches:
 A Devotional Anthology for Hekate
Queen of the Great Below:
 An Anthology in Honor of Ereshkigal
From Cave to Sky:
 A Devotional Anthology in Honor of Zeus
Out of Arcadia:
 A Devotional Anthology for Pan
Anointed:
 A Devotional Anthology for the Deities of the Near
 and Middle East
The Scribing Ibis:
 An Anthology of Pagan Fiction in Honor of Thoth
Queen of the Sacred Way:
 A Devotional Anthology in Honor of Persephone
Unto Herself:
 A Devotional Anthology for Independent Goddesses
The Shining Cities:
 An Anthology of Pagan Science Fiction

Forthcoming Titles

Shield of Wisdom:
A Devotional Anthology in Honor of Athena
Sirius Rising:
A Devotional Anthology for Cynocephalic Deities
Megaloi Theoi:
A Devotional for The Dioskouroi and Their Families
Harnessing Fire:
A Devotional Anthology in Honor of Hephaestus
Crossing the River:
An Anthology in Honor of Sacred Journeys

BIBLIOTHECA ALEXANDRINA

Lightning Source UK Ltd.
Milton Keynes UK
UKHW021426261022
411133UK00014B/2169

9 781480 228825